Learning to Learn

CAROLYN OLIVIER AND
ROSEMARY F. BOWLER

FOREWORD BY BILL COSBY

A FIRESIDE BOOK
PUBLISHED BY SIMON & SCHUSTER

FIRESIDE
Rockefeller Center
1230 Avenue of the Americas
New York, NY 10020

Designed by Irving Perkins Associates

Illustrations on pages 35, 36, 63, and 199 are by Martha Haas. The
Master Notebook page on page 189 is copyright © 1993 Landmark
College.

Manufactured in the United States of America

20 19 18 17 16 15 14 13 12

Library of Congress Cataloging-in-Publication Data

Olivier, Carolyn.
    Learning to learn / Carolyn Olivier and Rosemary F. Bowler ;
        foreword by Bill Cosby.
            p.   cm.
    "A Fireside book."
    Includes bibliographical references and index.
        1. Dyslexics—Education (Higher)—Vermont—Putney—Case
        studies.   2. Learning disabled—Education (Higher)—
        Vermont—Putney—Case studies.   I. Bowler, Rosemary F.,
        II. Title.
    LC4709.5.V52P885   1996   96–18548
    371.91'44—dc20   CIP

ISBN: 978-0-6848-0990-8

To Landmark's students . . .

whose honesty, energy, courage, thoughtfulness,
and sense of humor have filled many wonderful years
of work with joy and learning

C.O.

In memory of Eleanor Noyes
1908–1991

Teacher, poet, cheerleader, friend
who cherished the infinite variety that life offers
to those who laugh and think and keep on learning

R.F.B.

Acknowledgments

We thank our mentors, our colleagues, our students, our families, and our friends who have taught us to cherish the uniqueness of each person we encounter. We must share the credit with them if this book helps others to see the value of diversity in the way people view the world and learn from it.

For his inspiration, we thank the founder of Landmark College, Charles Drake, who dedicated his creativity and many years of his life to translating into practice his belief that students *can* learn those things that they find difficult.

We have had invaluable conversations with parents, grandparents, teachers, learning specialists, and adults with varied learning difficulties. They have encouraged our efforts, provided us with new insights, and made thoughtful comments and criticisms on one or more drafts of this work. Special thanks for their help to Malcolm Alexander, Kasha Barton, James Baucom, Brent Betit, Eleanor Boylan, Polly Bradley, Carolyn Cowen, Gloria Z. Davis, MacLean Gander, Ken Gobbo, Caroline Gumula, Linda Hecker, Leslie Hill, Betsy Hocker, Lynda Katz, Sandra Kleinman, Joyce Klucken, John Lappen, Mary Ann McCusker, Adrienne Major, Marge Meinke, Bill Morrison, Steve Nelson, Patrice Nolan, Christina Nova, Sheila Plank, Lou Salza, Sue

Shaffer, Dora Squatriti, Jane Thompson, Angela Wilkins, John Wilpers, Dianne Wood, and Susan Wood.

Many Landmark College students and their parents generously shared their experiences and their thoughts with us. In them we find the greatest hope for parents and students who may feel confused and alone. To all of them we are deeply grateful, as we are to other students and adults who have told us their stories. Except where full names are used, we have developed composite examples from the interviews we held while working on this book. Although not all students are named, we truly appreciate everyone who assisted us. Without their participation, we could not have presented the many examples of success that they have achieved, often despite many years of frustration.

We thank our editor, Sydny Miner, for her patience throughout the development and writing of this book, and for making our message clearer by suggesting important changes.

Special thanks also go to Anna and Peter Olivier, who have been understanding of Mom, "The Author," and who have provided firsthand experience on being a parent.

The dedication of Bill and Camille Cosby to the needs, the possibilities, and the accomplishments of all who approach life and learn in different ways inspired and sustained us while writing this book. We are especially indebted to Jim Olivier, Joel Brokaw, and Connie Newell for their commitment to the concepts on which this book is based, for the hours they spent critiquing and making suggestions for improvement, and above all, for believing in us when we needed it most.

C.O.
R.F.B.

Contents

Foreword

Hello. This is Bill Cosby, and I am supposed to write this Foreword. However, I know someone who has a wonderful life experience. I want him to . . . well, let him tell you.

"Russell, why does it take you so much time?"

When I was in school in the late forties and the fifties, teachers didn't know what to do with a child who needed more time. Soon came the next terrible question.

"Russell, what is wrong with you?"

What was wrong with me was that I felt incompetent, stupid, and dumb.

At the time, people just didn't know. So people would say, "He's nice but he's dumb." It was first a joke, but then soon parents didn't want their children around me because I was "dumb." I was put in a class of thirty students with all sorts of learning problems. Teachers didn't expect too much from us.

Often we would go on field trips—to plays, movies, zoos, or farms. Living in the city, all we would see were cats, dogs, or birds. That made it different, being on a farm, to see real horses and cows. Sometimes the farmer would show us how to milk cows and explain to us what it would take to run a farm, such as waking up in the wee hours of the morning to get eggs from the chickens. It was a lot of fun.

When the day was done, we had to return to school, and everything worsened when we had to face the other students. The fun was over. Back to name calling. Reality hit when the other children would make fun of the trip and what we had seen. And the teachers would ask us either to tell or draw pictures about what we liked at the farm. I couldn't draw well, but most of all I couldn't write about what I had seen. That made me feel double dumb.

In my class, the teacher only knew how to teach in an ordinary way. We had a reading book that had a lot of pictures and very few words. So the teacher would ask us to look at a picture and figure out the words. The teacher would ask, "So what do you think the word is?" and we would see the picture and say "jump." Then I went to a different school, where the reading books had no pictures. I couldn't read the words. By fifth grade, I couldn't read like the other kids. I felt ashamed because I didn't know how to syllabicate words. I fell into my own private world.

I will never forget one English teacher. Most of us were struggling, yet he told us that we would come out just fine. He told us to work at what we needed to do. At the time, we all thought he was crazy, but I will never forget him. Whenever I had a patient teacher and a smaller learning situation, it was always fruitful. But that only happened a very few times.

I knew if I had someone to take time with me, I could always learn. Why, I didn't know. I always kept a positive attitude. If you work with me and have patience with me, I can succeed. Even today, I don't like anyone hollering at me, or saying, "Why can't you do that?" I have a wall up against that.

Because my mother was working seventeen hours a day as a domestic and my father was often away serving as a career navy man, my parents did not have a lot of time to help me. I just said to myself that I would work hard to learn what I needed to be all right.

When I was thirteen years old, a teacher who was a friend of my mother's told her there was a trade school I could test for. I took the test and passed, and my mother agreed I could go.

The teaching was different in trade school. They showed and taught us at the right pace. We were involved in learning and it was a lot easier. The academic part was still hard, but I worked hard to achieve, because it was something I really wanted to do. I saw it as a source of how I could make a living. I knew I was capable of learning, and I learned many skills, but still I wasn't taught to read and write. After I graduated from trade school as an interior decorator, I was able to get a job. I married early, and started raising a family.

There was nothing I wouldn't do to get an education for my children. I was going to make sure my children could read and write. That was my goal. Because without these skills, there is really a negative side. Without reading and writing skills, you get lost in this world. My wife and I worked with our children. We stayed with them. We went into their schools. We got them tutors. They thought we were trolls at the time. But if they had a problem, our children knew we would work with them. Parents have to go and ask for help. We have to have pride in our hearts for our children and ask for help.

Parents take kids to church and to school. But it is not up to the preacher and the teacher to raise the child. It must come from home. We as parents have to make sure that our kids are being taught and that they are learning.

If we work with children to be educated and have self-respect, there are fewer problems, because then those children can be working for a goal. They won't have so much time to get involved in things like drugs. Once we give children support, they can be proud because of what they can do.

The teacher or the parent might say, "Let the children do it themselves." But who is going to give them the help to solve the problems they are having? Our job is to go to the teacher and find out what we can do to help. Because when children are having trouble and can't get help, we lose them. The children get frustrated and embarrassed and then begin to go to the back of the class and hope they don't get called on. Inside their minds, they wonder what is wrong.

Children need help from home. As parents, we can't just say to the child, "Why did you get a D?" or "Why did you get an F?" And we can't just ask that child to go and do it alone, because inside he or she is hurt. Other children can break down this child's self-esteem. I know this. You can be pushed out, to be by yourself as a loner. And that's not fair.

All of our three children graduated from high school and went to college. But there was something still on my mind that I always wanted to do—and that was to get an education. When my daughter graduated from Alabama A&M in Huntsville, there was a fellow that walked across the stage at the commencement with his chest stuck out like a proud rooster. He was fifty-eight years old. I said to myself, "I can do that." The same year, my nephew graduated from Columbia University in New York City, and in that class there was a seventy-three-year-old man who received his degree. I knew then that I could do it.

My nephew told me that he went to Landmark for one summer because he was having problems in college. He thought that the school could help me very much. So I went to Landmark to be tested, and I was diagnosed as dyslexic. I had never heard of it—I didn't know what dyslexia was. The Landmark counselor explained to me about different ways of learning, and I knew that I wanted to overcome my fears and pursue an education. I am a visual learner. And I need to know why and how each step must be done, in a very concrete way. Then I understand the concept of what I am doing.

On my first day of school, I was assigned to a tutor. One-on-one teaching with tutors is an important part of Landmark's methods. While I was walking to meet my tutor, everything came back. I thought, *Well, here we go again. When I get there, he's going to say, "What's wrong with you?" or "Why does it take you so long?"* The things I've heard all my life. But my tutor was very calm, and he didn't say too much. Then we started to work, and that broke the ice.

At fifty-two, you would think I'm going for my doctorate. This is the first time in my life I have been proud of what I have accomplished. I'm working hard. I'm doing well.

Within myself, I am very proud of where I am and what I've learned. My life has changed to the most fullness that it has ever been. It has taken me this long to realize that I can be taught, and that I can learn. I'm going to keep on pushing. And there isn't anything that's going to stop me.

Now! This Foreword will help you understand why this book is so important.

BILL COSBY

Introduction

If you are reading this book, chances are you are the parent of a child who is having trouble in school. Your son or daughter may be in elementary school or in college, but no matter how old your child is, you are worried about him. You are sure he is intelligent—he shows it in so many ways: He may have obvious artistic or mechanical ability. Perhaps he is a perceptive observer of people, of relationships, or of the natural world. This child of yours may be the one who sees the solutions to problems that arise in the home or the neighborhood. He may show poise and intelligence and grace on the soccer field or in dance class or on horseback. Your child often surprises you with his imagination and his creative ways of expressing that imagination in words, in colors, or with ideas.

But in spite of all the evidence you see each day of his intelligence, he is struggling to keep his head above water in school, or perhaps he has given up trying. Maybe he is spending more time in the principal's office than he is in the classroom, or perhaps he is withdrawn and unhappy. You may first question what is happening to this bright child of yours when he begins to make excuses to avoid going to school. He may complain of vague illnesses for which your doctor can find no physical basis. As he moves from grade to grade, you see that he is spending more time and struggling harder than his classmates but he seldom produces work that measures up to his capability.

This bright child of yours may look upon each September with all the hope and resolve that adults bring to listing their New Year's resolutions. Whether we resolve to diet, to give up smoking, or to exercise regularly, by the time March comes around, few of us can summon up the original enthusiasm we had for keeping these resolutions. We often become discouraged when keeping our promises to ourselves becomes a struggle, particularly when we fail to see the results we had hoped for.

Your child, seeing few successes in spite of his earnest desire to "make this year better," may become discouraged by midyear and count the days until this school year, too, has passed into history. With a succession of such experiences, this child who entered school happy and eager to learn may come to dread the start of school in September, or on each Monday morning. He may see himself in terms of his school performance, thinking of himself as "dumb," "unmotivated," or even as "bad."

Over the years, you and his teachers may have spent hours trying to solve the puzzle this child presents, subjecting him to batteries of tests and providing him with small-group or tutorial instruction, counseling, or any one of a number of special programs. None of this has produced a lasting change in your child's performance or in his feelings about himself. As a parent, you are baffled, frustrated, perhaps angry—and you feel alone.

But you are not alone. Countless caring parents each year confront the feelings of anxiety and concern that you have. We will meet a few such parents in Chapter 1 and listen to their stories. They are the parents of young adults who are enrolled in a summer program at Landmark College in Putney, Vermont. Landmark is the only fully accredited college in the United States founded specifically for students with learning disabilities. Its mission is to prepare such students to meet the demands of higher education and of the workplace. Since its founding in 1985, more than 80 percent of the graduates of its two-year program have gone on to successfully complete rigorous programs at many four-year colleges. Some have completed graduate schools. Others have specialized in the arts, in technology, and in the social services and now are employed and using their previously hidden abilities in ways they find rewarding, in ways that contribute to the communities and institutions in which they are working.

Landmark College is unique in its mission and in its curriculum, but the teaching principles it employs are those that good teachers have always recognized as effective ways to help all students succeed. Unfortunately, in a time of growing public concern about the quality of education, coupled with budget tightening, these sound teaching principles are often neglected. In spite of the many problems besetting schools and colleges today, many do provide effective services for students with learning problems, and a number of them apply the kinds of teaching and learning methods this book will describe. In fact, all schools and colleges are required by law to serve such students. The extent to which they do so and the quality and results of their programs range from grudging acceptance of the law to wholehearted endorsement of the value of unlocking the potential of all able students.

Landmark, however, in addition to being the only accredited college where enrollment is limited to students with learning problems, is unique in several other ways. Based on the belief that helping students develop the skills they need to succeed in higher education and in the workplace is its central responsibility, Landmark's admission process focuses not on prior grades and SAT scores but on identifying each applicant's learning strengths and weaknesses and determining how each student learns most efficiently. Once a student is admitted, teachers, tutors, and counselors devote significant amounts of time to helping each student to discover how he learns best and to appreciate the many normal variations in approaches to learning.

Perhaps the way in which Landmark differs most critically and most markedly from the majority of programs for students with learning problems is its focus on teaching students the language and study skills they find difficult. Developing these skills allows them to pursue further study or to enter the world of work with confidence. To promote such independence, students are taught, in a highly structured program, to rely on their own abilities rather than to depend on external supports, such as readers, scribes, and tape recordings.

Thus, recognizing that the principles of human development and of learning discussed in the chapters to come are those to which most thoughtful teachers and parents subscribe, we use the Landmark story as a model exemplifying these principles. Appendix A describes in detail the Landmark philosophy and the programs that put into practice the principles of teaching and learning presented throughout this book. Because it is the institution with which the authors have been most directly involved, we cite the experiences of Landmark students, faculty, and parents frequently in the pages that follow.

The Landmark story is one of hope, based on confronting difficulties and dealing with them. From the Landmark story, as told by students and parents, by teachers and counselors, we hope that you will discover that most students with learning problems can address these problems and that you will learn how this can be accomplished.

Chapter 1, Roundtable, sets the stage by introducing a group of Landmark parents and students and letting them share their thoughts. You will discover that many of their feelings and concerns are the same ones that have led you to seek answers for your child. Chapter 2, Many Ways to Learn, is divided into sections that describe the ways we learn by seeing, hearing, and doing and emphasizes the central role of language development in all learning. Chapter 3 compares several learning functions with the work carried on in a busy office and focuses on the roles of memory, attention, and automatization in learning. Each of these topics is explained by using familiar experiences and examples drawn from everyday life.

The theme of Chapters 2 and 3 is that there are many ways to learn, although not all are equally honored in school or on the job. Some of us, for example, learn most efficiently by relying on what we see, others rely on what we hear, some learn best by doing, and still others by using several learning channels at the same time. Because language is the basis for learning and living, the ways we learn to speak, to read, and to write are central concepts.

Throughout these chapters we stress that variations in learning are normal, we examine ways in which such variations may create problems in school, and we make recommendations for ways parents and teachers can help when problems occur. Traditionally, schools foster listening and reading as the main ways of learning. Bright students who learn more readily through other means—such as talking, building models, or drawing diagrams—may run into roadblocks as they move from elementary school to secondary school and on to college. In these chapters, students who learn differently describe their earlier school experiences and talk about how learning differently affected them and their academic performance.

Chapter 4, Interconnections and Chain Reactions, shows how variations in learning may lead a student toward later learning difficulties. Often early clues are quite clear but may seem unimportant. Thus, the learning problems they signal may go unrecognized and unaddressed. The emotional cost to the individual and the costs to society that can result if these clues are ignored are compelling reasons for examining interconnections and chain reactions.

Although most people who have gone through school have had experience in taking tests of ability and achievement, the world of testing can be baffling, even frightening. Chapter 5, Taking the Mystery Out of Testing, discusses the uses of such tests, outlines the procedures used by diagnosticians, describes what is involved in a good evaluation, and shows how test results can be used to plan an educational program.

Parents (teachers, as well) often seek specific guidelines for working with students who learn differently. Chapter 6, What Works in School, provides a detailed description of the teaching principles on which Landmark College bases its program. This includes locating the student's point of mastery in each academic area. The discussion of teaching principles is followed by a description of a structured, sequential approach to all course work through the use of a Master Notebook. Although the material described is designed for use by teachers, the concepts on which it is based are readily adaptable to suit almost all tasks involving learning, responsibility, and organization. Parents, employees, and other adults who suspect they lack the skills to perform at their highest level will all find that what works in school works at home and on the job as well.

Parents are the first and most important teachers children have. What happens in the home, from infancy through adulthood, plays a more significant role in our lives, for good or ill, than almost any other experience. In Chapter 7, In the Home, we present some concrete ways for parents to use the principles described in the earlier chapters and to help their children become better students and more productive citizens.

The goal of all education is the creation of independent lifelong learners. To approach this goal, students must know how they learn, what their aptitudes and deficiencies, strengths and weaknesses are, and how to use this self-knowledge as students, employees, friends, and family members. Chapter 8, The Independent Learner, discusses the power of self-understanding and the principles of effective self-advocacy.

Appendix A, as mentioned above, provides a look inside Landmark College as a model program. Appendix B provides sources of information for other programs and institutions. Appendix C includes a list of organizations that provide services for students, parents, and teachers.

Appendix D lists magazines and newsletters, and

Appendix E consists of a bibliography for those seeking further information about learning and learning problems. Appendix F contains information about videotapes and audiotapes.

Learning to Learn is written for parents, but throughout the book we have included suggestions for the teachers and schools, as well as for the parents and the home. We have done so because we strongly believe that parents will have the greatest success in helping their children when they are able to understand, evaluate, and support what is happening at school. As we emphasize throughout this book, children learn the most when they join with their parents and their teachers as an informed, mutually supportive team.

Learning to Learn focuses not on disabilities but on the abilities and possibilities every learner has. It describes and celebrates the many different ways in which we learn. We have attempted to make a number of sophisticated and technical concepts clear to those who are not professional educators or psychologists. In doing so, we have, of necessity, been selective and, at times, have greatly simplified those concepts. We have made a conscious effort to present them in plain English. Whenever the material requires using technical language, we define it when it is introduced.

To examine how we learn, to identify problem areas, and to suggest courses of action, we look at ways of learning as if each were a separate process or function. These divisions are artificial, but by making them we hope to demonstrate the range of teaching and learning possibilities open to all learners. Keep in mind the fact that all of these processes and functions develop simultaneously and are interrelated. Most learning problems encompass more than one channel (such as vision) and function (memory), and thus we need to see each in relationship to all of the others.

No book or series of books can ever substitute for the skills professionals bring to bear on learning problems. If you question whether you or your child has learning needs, do not depend on what we say here alone. Seek help from those best qualified to provide it—your child's teachers, your family doctor, an educational or clinical psychologist, or another specialist.

1. Roundtable

> Standardization is for factories, not for schools. It is okay to reject bad products in the factory. But something major is wrong when kids get treated like factory rejects.
>
> Bill

Eagerness, fear, despair, bewilderment, sadness, guilt. These emotions are so strong that we can almost touch them in the group of fifty parents who meet on a July morning at Landmark College in the Green Mountains of Vermont. They are strangers to one another, but not to these feelings. They come from all across the country, from Texas and Florida, from Michigan and Ohio, from Wisconsin and Connecticut. They are African-American, Caucasian, Indian, Latino, Jewish, Christian, Muslim. There is an attorney, a policeman, a psychiatrist, a secretary, a chemical engineer, an anthropologist, a plumber, a single parent on welfare. Their children have attended struggling inner-city schools, suburban public and parochial schools, and elite private schools. What these parents have in common is that each has a son or daughter with a learning disability, and these students are all attending a rigorous summer program at

Landmark. With this strong common bond, the group diversity in gender, race, and class is forgotten.

In a round table—hesitantly at first, and then with increasing assurance as we move around the circle—these parents share their stories, each different, yet all in important ways the same.

Mrs. Z., a nurse who works with young cancer patients, relates the saga of her middle child, David, a creative boy caught between two high-achieving sisters. When David was thirteen, his older sister said, "David is going to get lost at the water fountain," thus giving voice to Mrs. Z.'s growing realization that her son was falling farther and farther behind in his schoolwork. As Mrs. Z. recalls, "David was a bright little boy, easy to get along with, who had a great imagination. But even as a young child, he would escape into a world of fantasy, especially when he faced a task that didn't make sense to him—or that didn't interest him. Losing himself in daydreams, he often did not hear me or his teachers. We all urged him to 'pay attention,' sometimes pretty abruptly and impatiently. It wasn't until his sister made that observation that I realized that we needed to find out why such a smart boy was having such a hard time in school."

Mr. A. shakes his head and chimes in, "Jim got by on his basic intelligence, good looks, and charm all the way through high school. He was a good kid, everyone liked him, so he got at least C's and sometimes B's without much effort. We knew he was capable of more, and so did his teachers. Together, over the years, we reinforced our belief that Jim's mediocre performance was the result of his own willful decision to goof off. We all fell into the 'blame the victim' trap. When he got to college, he discovered that the old charm didn't impress his professors."

"Well," Ms. M. interjects, "I knew Susan was falling behind her classmates by the time she hit fourth grade, but we could never get any help for her in school. They said she didn't qualify—she was not far enough behind for special help. I still get so angry when I think about it. What kind of a nation are we anyway if we accept the idea that a child has to fail and feel miserable before she can get help?"

"And," Mrs. Q. asks, "what are we thinking when we let students go on from grade to grade without ever asking them to meet any reasonable standards? I think we are failing our children, actually being dishonest, when we let them think that they can go through life with little effort and poorly developed skills. According to Dick, he never had more than twenty minutes of homework to do; he certainly never spent more time than that. He never had to write essays—which is just as well, since no one taught him the basics of writing. But Dick got decent grades. He thought, and so did we, that he was an okay student. It wasn't until he got to college that he found out he just couldn't hack it. He didn't know how to study, his reading was at an eighth-grade level, and his writing and spelling were awful. It was a real blow to his ego—and to ours, too—to find out we had all been living in never-never land for twelve years. We've got to start being honest with ourselves and with our children."

Ms. M. reenters the conversation. "I can see that your Dick and my Susan have different problems. I want to cry when I think of how hard Susan tried for so long, even when everyone was telling her she'd do fine if she'd just work harder. By the time she got to high school, she had stopped trying. I think she figured that if no one believed that she really was trying, there was no point in continuing. She concentrated on being popular, and because she was so agreeable, she managed to scrape by. But she often put herself down, saying she was just not a good student, that she was pretty stupid in school."

Mr. T., the policeman from a Boston suburb, has been waiting for a chance to jump into the discussion. "You know, I am having a hard time listening to all of you. My son has been filled with rage since he was in elementary school. He was always being sent to the office because he was disrupting the class. Of course, he never finished his work. Once when he was being disciplined, he jumped out the window in the principal's office. My wife and I practically lived at the school. He had a couple of great teachers who really cared about him and tried to help him and us, but none of us really had a clue about what he needed. I was ashamed that my son was acting like a child from a home where no one cared."

These voices of pain express the suffering of loving parents who, consciously or not, realistically or not, often see themselves at the root of their children's failures. Many of you may have similar stories to tell.

Mrs. Z. ended the session on an upbeat note: "Whatever has happened in the past, we can't change. But we can influence the future of our children for the better. All of us now know that there are reasons why bright students perform poorly in school. What I have learned over the past seven years is that my son can learn and can be successful. What he needs is teachers who are consistent, demanding, and thorough, and who understand the ways he learns best."

If the stories told by the parents who met in Vermont strike a familiar chord, if you hear your own feelings expressed in some of their voices, you may have a David, a Susan, a Jim, or a Dick in your family. How can you tell? What difference does it make? What can be done about it? These and other questions will be addressed in the chapters that follow.

But before we turn to answer those questions, let's listen to some students. How do they feel? How have their school problems affected them? The voices are those of young adults, college-age and older.

"It would be a lot easier to live with the fact that I have trouble learning if this made me look different," declares Eric. "If you wear glasses, people accept the fact that you have poor eyesight; if you use a cane or crutches, people realize that you are coping with some kind of disability. But when you have a learning problem, people think you are lazy or stupid or that you just don't care. If people could see inside my head and recognize that I am smart and I am trying, they would handle it differently."

When differences are visible and obvious, no matter how difficult they may be to endure, most parents and teachers seek understanding and treatment. When they cannot see such differences, however, they may misinterpret and misunderstand the behavior they see. If Eric—who demonstrates his intelligence in his articulate analyses of music and the arts, his dramatic talents, and his understanding of modern poetry—fails to achieve as his parents and teachers expect him to in school, they may well assume that it is because he is lazy, unmotivated, or turned-off.

At twenty-five, Mary Jo is a poised young woman who speaks passionately about her past. Because she was having such a hard time learning to read, her parents sent her to a private school for several years. "That school," she says, "taught me how to be social, how to be a good leader. It fostered my self-esteem and taught me lots of life skills. I had a great time there and felt good about myself. The only problem—and of course I didn't see it at the time—was that I wasn't learning to read and write. In school, everyone thought I was cute. I was small and blond and a great runner. I was known as the dizzy jock. When I finally realized how much trouble I was in, I was in college and failing. I enrolled in a special study-skills and reading program and discovered that I was reading at a third-grade level."

And with tears in her eyes and in a trembling voice, Mary Jo cries out, "I shouldn't have gotten so far before I found the help I needed. Why was I shoved along the assembly line, never knowing how little I knew? How could I graduate without anyone realizing that I did not know how to study, how to organize, how to take notes? These are not skills we are born knowing. And they are not skills that are all that difficult to learn. But I needed someone to teach them to me, and teach them over and over until I mastered them. I don't understand why every student does not get this kind of instruction and have to meet standards based on these skills in every school, in every grade. It's a crime!"

Tom, a junior in a liberal arts college, talks about discovering for himself that his inability to devise efficient study habits was eroding his confidence. The longer and harder he studied, with no plan of attack, the less successful he was. Taking a summer and a full academic year out of his college program to tackle his learning problems has given him renewed enthusiasm for striving to reach his goal of becoming a historian, which will demand massive amounts of reading, organization, research, and writing.

Bob proves to be both insightful and highly verbal. "By the time I was twenty-one, I figured that I'd probably spend my life as a bartender, if I was lucky enough to hold a job. I was trying to make it through a community-college program but failing miserably. One day I was hanging around the learning center when they came looking for volunteers to take a test. I figured it wouldn't hurt. After they scored the test, they came back and said, 'There is a reason you are failing, and it is not lack of intelligence. You need help to make use of that intelligence.'

"I was lucky enough to find the world's best teacher to tutor me in English and math. The first semester I worked with her, I hated it. She was on my case all the time, so I spent a lot of time complaining and feeling sorry for myself. Then one day I realized that I had written a three-page report, something I'd never done before. A little later I got a B on an algebra exam. All the structure, the consistency, the fact that she made me follow a set pattern for reading and note taking and organizing a Master Notebook began to make sense. I still have a lot of personal problems, and I am getting help from a counselor. But I truly believe you've got to get on the right track for learning before you can do anything about the rest of your life. I don't know what I will do next, but I do know that I'm not going to spend my life as a bartender."

Dan is entering his third year of law school. He had always known that he had trouble with organization, but both he and his parents thought he was just lazy. He shakes his head as he asks, "Can you believe that I went through twelve years of elementary and high school and four years of college and it wasn't until I got to law school that I ever heard about the basic building blocks of organized writing—topic sentences, main ideas, summary sentences? I don't see any reason why most of these skills couldn't be taught at much earlier grades."

A scholarship student in the summer program, Nicole says, "It always took me longer to do schoolwork than anyone else. I always needed tutors and special help. All through school, teachers complained that I talked too much, that I didn't try hard enough. But when you're putting your all into your work and people tell you to try harder, you begin to think, *What's the use?*"

Mary Jo, Jim, Bob, David, Susan, Dan, Tom, and Nicole all learn in nontraditional ways. Each is a unique person, no two have had the same experiences. Some of them discovered that they don't learn easily when they were in the primary grades; others never suspected that they had a learning problem until they reached college or graduate school. Each of them has at least average intelligence as measured by traditional IQ tests (more on this in Chapter 5) and as demonstrated by their success in areas such as art, music, sports, leadership, mechanics—all of which depend on the ability to think critically and creatively and to define and solve problems using visual, spatial, or interpersonal intelligence.

Although they all have histories of school-related problems, each has unique gifts as well. Many bright students who do not live up to expectations in school do learn to read at least adequately, although often slowly and inefficiently. Some, disturbing as it is to realize, graduate from high school with the reading skills of the average third-, sixth-, or eighth-grader. Few of them have had the opportunity to develop the step-by-step skills on which clear, well-organized, informative writing depend, or the study habits that will allow them to be lifelong learners.

So we have parents who have watched their children struggle for years, and students who have come to believe that they must be lazy or stupid. Although we have not heard from them yet, we have teachers who question themselves when they are unable to reach students they know are able. All these people are in search of answers, alternatives, and a better tomorrow.

This book is about parents, about their children, and about learning. We explain what is involved in learning, what hurdles must be cleared in the process. We talk about learning problems, how they can be identified, and how they can be overcome. We encourage you to think about yourselves, your child, and the learning process in new ways. If your child is struggling in school (or has given up the battle), you owe it to him, to yourself, and to the larger community to give him the key that opens the doors of opportunity.

This book is based on several beliefs: We believe that all parents—from whatever cultural, ethnic, or economic background—want their children to lead productive and satisfying lives. Parents hope that their children will have opportunities that they themselves have not had. Parents are their child's earliest teachers and most careful observers. They know their child is intelligent, but when that child runs into roadblocks in learning, parents react in many different ways. Some blame the other parent or the school. Others misunderstand the child's behavior, punishing him or insisting that if he really wanted to get good grades he could. Still others seek advice from teachers, counselors, pediatricians, relatives, and friends. Sometimes they get conflicting responses, which raise more questions than they answer. All of these are normal responses. Most parents need time and good information before they can deal realistically and humanely with their confusion, disappointment, frustration, anger, denial, or guilt.

First, such parents need to learn what learning is all about. Most of us drive automobiles every day without the foggiest notion of how an internal-combustion engine works. But if our car stalls frequently, we may decide that we need to learn more about engines. In like fashion, most of us go through school ourselves and then send our children off to learn without much, if any, knowledge of what is happening when people learn. Unless we are educators or psychologists, there is usually no compelling need for us to understand how we receive, process, store, and retrieve information.

But just as we might be motivated to learn more about the inner workings of our car if it malfunctions frequently, we will be most successful in helping a child who is stalled in learning if we focus on understanding the root causes of his difficulty rather than on our frustrations with his poor performance.

When our car fails us, we might in a moment of frustration kick the tires or swear at it. But we know that this will not solve the problem. We know, rationally, that the car is not deliberately letting us down. When our children face learning problems, it is easy to misunderstand or blame them. But like the car, they are not trying to annoy or anger us. Children and learning, infinitely more deserving of our understanding than cars, benefit from every effort we make on their behalf to understand their difficulties in school.

In the chapters that follow, we will examine in some detail the nature of the learning process, especially as it applies to students who have trouble learning in traditional ways. We will look at ways of determining how such students learn best, at the principles of instruction that have proved to be highly successful for such students, and at the pivotal role parents play in providing realistic support for their child as they guide him to become an independent learner and a self-reliant person.

2. Many Ways to Learn

Nora is in her first year at Landmark College. She is eager and enthusiastic. Her eyes sparkle and her whole body is engaged as she talks.

> I never thought at all before about how I learn best. I just figured that I wasn't much good at learning at all. One of the first things I learned when I met with an admissions counselor here was that I needed to really understand how my mind works before I would be able to make the best use of it. What's great is that no one here takes anything for granted. My tutor and the study-skills teacher spend a lot of time helping me to figure out how I learn.

WHAT KIND OF LEARNER ARE YOU?

Have you ever analyzed how you approach new tasks or learn new skills? Can you concentrate in the midst of noise and confusion, or do you have to find a quiet place when you are doing a task that is complex or detailed? Do you learn better by reading, by listening, by watching, by questioning and discussing, by taking notes, by

doing, or by using several of these learning channels?
Do you rely on one method of learning for some new
tasks and a different method for others?

When you confront a new task, such as preparing a
budget, or you decide to learn a new skill, such as a
foreign language, do you dive right in and immerse
yourself? Or do you spend some time examining the
task or skill, deciding what to do first, getting together
the materials you expect to need, reading directions,
and asking questions?

Imagine that you have to set up a new computer
either in your home or office. Which of these approaches do you think would be most efficient for you
to use?

1. Reading the manual as you unpack the computer
   and following its directions step by step as you
   attempt to set it up;
2. Reading the manual for setting up the computer
   and then observing a colleague, so you can relate
   what he does to the directions in the manual;
3. Carefully watching an experienced friend set up
   a similar computer, noticing the order in which
   he completes each step and seeing where the
   cables and plugs go and how the printer and
   accessories are attached;
4. Asking your colleague questions as he is setting
   up the computer about the order in which he
   takes the steps and about the purpose of the
   various cables;
5. Setting up the computer without referring either
   to another person or to the manual but instead
   relying on your past experience, your general
   knowledge, and what makes sense to you;

6. Taking notes or writing out in sequence the steps you need to take to complete the task;
7. Drawing pictures or diagrams to guide you before you start to set up the computer;
8. Repeating directions and talking through the process to yourself, either mentally or out loud, as you perform the steps ("Now I am connecting the printer cable to Port A").

In choosing your approach, you are consciously or unconsciously picking one or more channels for learning to provide you with the information you need to carry out this task. There is no absolute right or wrong approach; there is only a best way for you, depending on which of your "learning channels" work most efficiently.

Let's look at how these different channels promote learning. What are some of the most important learning channels and how do they function? We will begin by examining what we learn from what we see, hear, and do. We will also discuss the reasons that students who don't learn equally well in each of these channels run into problems in school. Often the problem lies not within the student but in our limited knowledge of the normal range of variations in learning.

Learning from What We See

I am a strong visual learner. When I study, I am not aware only of words in the text, but I use pictures, diagrams, and graphs to help me understand the content of the assignment. I make associations with things I already know by making mental pictures as I read and recalling the visual images I have stored in my mind that relate to what I am studying.

Kelly

Much of what we learn comes to us through our eyes. Taking in images from the world around us—vision—is the first step. But learning from what we see requires more than just vision. Learning depends on the interaction of vision with the brain's system for deriving and storing meaning. Let's take a look at the development of some important functions necessary for learning from what we see.

VISUAL LEARNING SKILLS IN INFANCY AND EARLY CHILDHOOD

From the moment of birth, the infant's eyes are taking in information. At first the baby distinguishes light and dark, colors, general shapes, and motion. As vision becomes more acute, he begins to see variations in shape, size, and color and to recognize the people and objects that make up his world. He begins to notice essential details. A very important brain process is under way as the baby recognizes and categorizes what he sees, basing his new understanding on his growing ability to see similarities and differences. The baby comes to recognize that Kris, the family's pet elkhound, is like the neighbor's springer spaniel in overall appearance but very different in individual features—different in size, color, shape of head, coat, tail.

As the baby and young child meet up with more and more dogs, their perception of "dogginess" becomes more firmly established. They form a visual understanding of the general features that make a dog different from other animals. They develop the ability to recognize that the elkhound, the springer spaniel, the golden retriever, and the dachshund are all dogs. Each shape brings the idea of a dog to the child. When he has this sense of the whole, he can identify a dog even when he can see only part of it—for example, when it is lying under the table with only its tail sticking out. This sense of the whole, or the outside shape of something, is called **gestalt perception.**

Young children also begin to recognize important details and make increasingly sophisticated discriminations. Before long they can distinguish Mickie from Max in a litter of look-alike puppies. Making these fine distinctions between things that are similar in appearance is called **visual discrimination.**

Although he may see an object, such as a rattle, from only one side or angle, the baby begins to understand the object in terms of its three dimensions. In other words, he recognizes the rattle, even when its position, location, or orientation changes. He notices people and may observe, *Pete is big, but when I see him walking down the street he looks smaller and smaller.* **Object constancy**—understanding what an object looks like independent of its distance, location, and position—is a concept acquired in infancy. The baby's rattle is a rattle no matter which way he turns it. Pete is Pete no matter how near or far away he is, whether he is sitting, lying down, or standing on his head.

At a very early age, the infant also shows evidence of something called **recognition memory.** When Kris trots into the room, the baby's facial expression and body movements all seem to say, *I know who you are. I've seen you before. I recognize you.*

For a short time in infancy, Kris is only in the baby's consciousness when he can see her. At this stage, his sister may take his rattle from his crib to put it away, or Kris may leave the room. While the infant may notice these disappearances briefly, he soon forgets the existence of the rattle or of Kris. This "out of sight, out of mind" stage does not last long. The child soon understands that things exist even when he can't see them. In addition, repeated exposure to the people and objects in his world strengthens his ability to picture things that aren't actually in front of him. Kris may be outside playing or sleeping in the next room out of the baby's sight, yet he knows that his dog is there, and he can call her image to mind. The child's growing understanding of his world, supported by his increasing ability to visualize what he has previously seen, establishes the basis for his **visual memory.**

Relationships, Patterns, and Organization

As the child makes sense of the array of visual information that reaches him, he learns how the things he sees are arranged in space. He notices the arrangement of chairs around the kitchen table. He watches Dad assemble the blender to make frozen fruit shakes, and he notices all the parts (jar, lid, base, blade, seal, and screw) that make up the blender. He begins to see things in relation to one another and to understand the nature of these relationships.

The child discovers other visual patterns of order and organization in his environment. Coats, each on its own hanger, fill the hall closet. On the cabinet shelf, objects that are alike—cups, plates, bowls—are piled together. Family photographs are centered on the wall and hung according to the years in which they were taken. The nine players on the baseball team make a distinctive formation on the playing field. The ability to recognize and understand such patterns is an important component of organizational skill.

Unique Aspects of Visual Learning

A key feature of the preschooler's visual learning system is that for the most part, until he closes his eyes at bedtime, the child can look, explore, and examine things again and again, as long as he likes. Although there are some visual experiences that are time-limited (for example, watching Kris disappear as she chases a cat down the street), for the most part "seeing" is self-directed. The child can examine his rattle as long as he wants. He can play with it for one minute or for thirty minutes.

Another distinctive feature of the visual system is the ability to perceive simultaneously many features of the visual environment. When the child watches Kris chase a cat down the street, he registers the cars and trucks on the street, the trees, the sidewalk, and the children walking to school. If he goes out to look for Kris, he may later talk more about the puddles in the street than anything else he has seen.

NETWORKING INFORMATION

The discussion so far has been concerned solely with learning from what we see. The senses do not operate in isolation, however. Right from the start, the infant's brain is networking information taken in through all the senses.

Early in life the infant begins to make associations between the information he takes in through his eyes and information he receives through his other senses: touching, hearing, tasting, smelling, doing. Information from what he sees and does is networked as the baby reaches out to touch what he sees. Before the baby can use words for thinking or expressing his thoughts, his eyes give his hands the nonverbal feedback that tells him, *I'm near that Cheerio. I've almost got it. I've got it!* Infants also learn what things feel like and what the functions and purposes of objects and actions are. As they do so, they enhance their visual skills and refine their motor skills. They continue throughout infancy and childhood to develop their visual-motor skills through such activities as catching a ball, drawing, cutting, and writing.

Children also begin to make associations between the information their eyes take in and the information that comes through their ears. The first such association many babies make is putting together Mother's face and her voice. Later, he may associate Kris, the family dog, with the sound of her bark or with the scratching sound her paws make on the linoleum floor. Even before the baby can talk, he may show that he has learned the dog's name by looking for her when asked, "Where's Kris?"

Most young children are relentlessly curious— pointing to objects and asking, "What is that?" or continually wanting to know "How?" and "Why?" They develop a network of information about the world they live in, learning names and words for living things, objects, places, categories, characteristics, functions, and actions. We will say much more about language learning later. What it is important to remember here is that the child, with everything he sees and with every movement and sound he makes or takes in, is making associations, "networking," among the many pieces of information he receives.

VISUAL LEARNING IN SCHOOL: NEW CHALLENGES

When he enters the world of school, the child faces many new tasks that require him to make sense of what he sees. Some tasks build on the visual skills the child has developed in the preschool years; others require him to master new visual skills so that he will understand the new things he is seeing.

Discrimination in the Environment

The first challenge school presents is the need to discriminate differences in an environment where many objects look alike. In entering this new world, the child faces a number of practical demands that he will meet easily or with difficulty, depending on his ability to make visual discriminations. He must be able to find his classroom, his locker, his lunch box, his school bus, and his parents' car in the parking lot. Most objects in each of these categories are quite similar in appearance, function, and design. Yet the child must be able to see the "just noticeable differences" that distinguish his school bus, for example, in a line of vehicles that look almost alike.

Most children are careful observers of their environment and have little difficulty making these discriminations. For those children who persistently confuse similar-appearing objects, however—such as pieces of clothing, classrooms, school buses, and lunch boxes—starting school can be confusing, anxiety-producing, surprising, and even frightening. Parents can do much to help the child who has this difficulty.

1. Parents can take the child on a tour of the building before he starts school and help him locate the bathrooms, the water fountains, the office, and the spot where he will be picked up at the end of the day. They can also reassure the child by pointing out that he does not need to know everything about the layout of the school by saying, for example, "You don't need to know how to get to the gym, because your teacher will take the entire class there as a group." Spending time rehearsing how to ask for help is another way to build his confidence.

2. Both parents and teachers can help children discriminate among similar objects by pointing out several important distinguishing features. If the child only learns, "Your bus is the fourth one in line," he's bound to run into trouble the first time weather or scheduling problems interfere with the usual order. But if he has learned several key features that point out potential identification problems, the task becomes easy. "The bus is Number 72. That's a key feature. (There's also a bus Number 27, so be sure to look for the one that starts with 7.) The bus is usually the fourth one in line. The regular driver is a red-haired woman."

3. Both to make visual discrimination easier and to establish a foundation for organization skills, we

recommend identifying personal possessions and educational materials clearly, using labels, artwork, cartoons, covers, tape, or similar marks. There are many visual discrimination tasks in the early school years, and all children can gain from simple practices such as these. They are especially important for the child who has trouble making these distinctions.

4. Most children will improve their discrimination skills as they have more experience talking about what they see and developing their observational skills by describing and explaining. At first, parents may need to guide these discussions and point out the key features. Later, they can ask questions to guide the students to draw their own conclusions ("How can you make sure that you will recognize your skates at the rink?"). This kind of verbalizing helps students develop an internal voice, which can guide their eyes to pay attention to the distinguishing features of the environment.

Discriminating Letters, Numbers, and Symbols

The most important visual discrimination challenge for children when they start school is learning the symbols involved in reading and writing. They must learn to recognize and distinguish between similar-looking letters (*a/o, v/u, r/n, m/n*) and words (*that/what, house/ horse, unclear/nuclear*). Such fine distinctions are necessary for learning to read and write.

Children must also recognize the essential similarity in the shape (gestalt) of letters and other symbols. For example, they must identify the letter *g* whether it is in their teacher's flowing cursive, the print in their workbook, their own writing, or their neighbor's scrawl. Despite the superficial differences in these four presentations, children need to see that they are all the letter g. When they receive a poor photocopy of an assignment, they may be expected to read what is written on the page, even though the words are faint or incomplete.

Most preschoolers and many first- and second-grade children have some difficulty discriminating between similar letters. They sometimes will reverse numbers and letters as well. Although young children frequently display these problems, most of them are resolved as children have repeated exposure to reading and writing activities. Children who have age-appropriate language skills and strengths in other areas usually learn to compensate for deficiencies in visual discrimination and become good readers. Fortunately, there are many ways to help children with such difficulties, several of which we suggest below.

1. Provide frequent opportunities for the child to call on as many senses as possible when working with symbolic language. By seeing, saying, and doing, he will begin to compensate for weakness in visual discrimination by calling on strengths in other areas. Such practice is called multisensory teaching, an approach that has a well-deserved reputation for helping children succeed in learning to read.

2. Encourage the child to use his motor system to reinforce visual learning. Many people with visual impairments capitalize on their sense of touch and develop an unusually strong sense of spatial relations. Tracing or writing letters on a

rough surface, such as a rug or a piece of Masonite, is good practice for students whose visual discrimination is poor. Some young children respond positively to practice that involves handling and tracing large letters cut from sandpaper.

3. Encourage children to use oral language to describe what they see. As they talk, help them identify key features by asking questions and engaging in discussion. When they describe what the letters *a, q, p,* and *b* have in common and the ways in which those letters differ, they are supporting visual discrimination skills required for reading with accuracy and understanding.

Which Way Is the Right Way?

By the time they enter school, most children know that objects in the three-dimensional world do not change their identity when they are turned to a different position (object constancy). When children draw a picture of a three-dimensional object, such as a chair, on a flat piece of paper, they may orient the object any way they please. But the symbols they learn in school follow a different rule. In the flat, two-dimensional world of school paper work, orientation and directionality are very important. In fact, the differences between *b/d, p/q,* and +/× are defined solely by their orientation in space. To read, write, and spell, children must understand and remember these distinctions.

Much has been written about the child who has trouble remembering the difference between *b*'s and *d*'s and who seems to read and write letters and numbers

backwards. Distinguishing between such letters is a
special kind of visual discrimination task. There are
many multisensory activities to help children of different ages resolve this difficulty. One such exercise uses
the word *bed*, the image of a bed, and the child's language and motor systems. First, have the child make a
fist with his left hand and raise his forefinger.

In doing so, he forms the shape of the letter *b*. When he
then repeats the exercise with his right hand, that hand
forms the letter *d*. Next, ask the child to bring his two
fists together so that the fingers on each hand are touching. He has now created a shape that looks like a bed,
complete with headboard and foot board, an object that
he is familiar with.

This three-dimensional shape represents a word
that starts with *b* (a letter with a loop on the right) and
ends with *d* (a letter with a loop on the left). Engage in
discussion as he performs this exercise, and have him
pronounce the word and associate the letter sounds
with the symbols.

This simple exercise gives children a tool for
quickly determining whether the letter that they see or
need to remember is *b* or *d*. They may rely on this

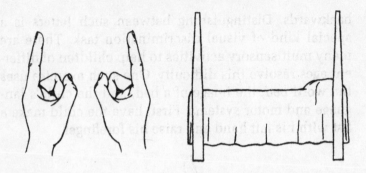

reminder as long as they need to, using their hands under their desks and casually glancing down at the "bed."

Visual Memory

Teachers and parents may not be aware of how much school learning depends on the child's ability to remember information that he sees.

Reading and Spelling

Learning letters and words, and using them to read and spell, is one of the earliest and most demanding visual memory tasks. Remembering individual symbols, or a sequence of symbols, "in the mind's eye" is much more difficult than most adults realize.

Many children can close their eyes, picture their best friend in their mind, and describe or draw what they see. But it is a different task to picture the word *friend* and then to spell it aloud or to write it. Both tasks involve visual memory, but spelling, which requires remembering a sequence of symbols, is a far more difficult memory task for most young children. A child may be able to visualize people and situations easily but have a hard time retrieving from his memory the symbols required for spelling and writing. Thus a verbal and creative child who has a rich store of ideas and memories, but who has trouble remembering symbols, may become frustrated when he has to write a description of his friend.

A child with a good **recognition memory** for symbols may read the word *friend* correctly when he sees it but still have trouble spelling it from memory when it is not in front of him. Students like this are often excellent readers but poor spellers.

Different Methods, Different Demands

Many schools today rely on either the "sight word" approach or the "whole language" approach for teaching young children to read and spell. "Sight word" instruction requires young children to learn and memorize new words based on their visual appearance (the outside shape of the word and the sequence of letters within). "Whole language" approaches are based on the belief that just as children learn to talk naturally and without direct instruction, they will learn to read and to enjoy reading naturally by being exposed to good literature. This method, too, capitalizes on students' ability to learn and remember words "by sight."

Less frequently used and quite different in philosophy are the "phonics" and "code emphasis" methods, which use individual letters and their sounds, and word patterns, as the building blocks for teaching children to read by "decoding" unfamiliar words. These methods do not make as many demands on a child's visual memory for symbols, or "sight learning."

There are also tasks other than reading and writing

that involve memory for symbols, or sight learning. These include remembering formulas, charts, and tables (such as the periodic table of elements) in mathematics and the sciences.

Here are some ways to help students become better readers and spellers by using other learning channels to support visual memory:

1. Since most school programs concentrate on the shape of words, rather than on the structure of language, children who have problems in learning to read "by sight" should receive instruction in language rules and patterns. Many excellent multisensory methods and materials exist for this purpose. If students of any age have the chance to learn and practice reading and spelling rules and patterns using these techniques, they need not go through life as inadequate readers and spellers. The organizations listed in Appendix C can provide information about specific multisensory programs.

2. Computer "spell checks" supply several spellings for incorrect words that appear in a document. Students with good recognition memory can usually pick out the correct spelling without having to generate it entirely from memory.

3. Students at higher levels who are allowed to refer to sheets containing key formulas in math and science can focus on the content of the assignment, rather than struggling to retrieve this information from memory.

4. For all students, but especially for those who find remembering symbols troublesome, icon-based word-processing programs give some ad-

vantage. The pictorial representations of a desk-top, filing cabinets, trash cans, and other familiar objects help to simplify tasks and to give students time to concentrate on the important aspects of their work.

Copying from the Chalkboard

Students also must rely on visual memory when they have to copy material from the chalkboard, from slides, or from projection screens to their paper. They work efficiently to the extent that they can memorize and hold "chunks" of symbolic information in their minds as they work.

Copying from the chalkboard is a common problem for students whose visual memory for symbols is limited and who have not developed other ways to remember the information in chunks. Children who can absorb only small chunks of information are the ones who are looking back and forth from their paper to the material they are copying, working slowly or inaccurately, perhaps omitting or confusing information.

Speed of processing becomes an increasingly important issue for high school and college students. During preschool years and in situations outside the classroom, children usually can look at things as long as they like. In school, this is often not possible. Especially at upper levels, schoolwork requires students to process visual information with increasing speed. They are expected to complete tasks such as copying assignments from the chalkboard or reading from a text within a limited amount of time. This demand for increasing speed places an added burden on students who have difficulty remembering what they see.

There are several ways teachers can minimize the problems that students encounter when they must copy from the chalkboard.

1. Use handouts to reduce the need for copying.
2. Give the gift of time so that students can copy with care and check what they have copied.
3. Be sure that visual presentations of any kind are clear and well organized, with adequate margins, and that they have enough empty space to reduce visual confusion.
4. Accompany visual presentations with clear verbal explanations.
5. Allow the student to check his notes for completeness after class, using the teacher's materials or the notes of a designated student.
6. Teach memory strategies, such as "chunking," described in the "Memory" section of this book (see pages 109–110.)

Visual and Spatial Organization

Without direct instruction, some children see and understand how words and sentences are organized into paragraphs on pages with margins and how numbers are aligned in columns and math problems are laid out in their workbooks. They know how to space their work evenly across a page by observing how it is done in books and worksheets. They see how books are arranged on a shelf and organize books in their desks and lockers in a similar way. Such children have made sense of what they see. They understand visual-spatial organization, and by practicing what they see, they develop an important tool for school success.

Children whose environment lacks visual and spatial organization or who do not see how to organize it may find even the simplest tasks overwhelming. They may become frustrated when they have to clean out their desks or lockers, or when they have to follow a particular format for a written assignment. They may have little idea about how to organize either new or familiar items, and they often depend on their memory, rather than on a system, to locate things. These children need help in discovering ways to organize visually and spatially, whether they are dealing with a page of math problems or with the clutter they accumulate in and on the desks where they do their homework. When they come to see structure in this world, they can approach their potential for learning.

For all but those who have excellent organizational abilities, some degree of disorganization or messiness is normal. Although a few students work well in what appears to be a mass of disorganized materials, most benefit from implementing a systematic approach for organizing their materials and their assignments. They can be taught how to use their eyes, to observe patterns around them, and to model their own work on these structures and arrangements.

There are a number of steps that parents and teachers can take to help students do a better job of organizing their physical environments.

1. Look through catalogues and visit stores with educational materials to locate products that promote systematic organization. Book bags, desk organizers, notebook dividers and pockets, filing and labeling systems, hole punchers, and staplers all help students to organize their materials.

2. We live in such a busy and cluttered world that we not only have to organize it but to simplify it as well, to reduce confusion as much as possible. Parents and teachers can help students identify what is important and what is not, what to save and what to throw away. Allocating time regularly—weekly, rather than once a month or semester—to clean out desks at home and at school tells students that adults recognize the relationship between being organized and making decisions about the value of accumulated materials.

3. Teachers and parents may place a low priority on the need to teach children organizational techniques directly, explicitly, and positively. Cleanup time in school may be relegated to the last few minutes of the class period at best, or it may not be provided at all. At home, the child may view cleaning his room or helping with household chores as a punishment. In fact, sometimes parents do use these chores to punish. This puts organization in a negative context and doesn't teach children its value. To help children develop and respect organizational skills, parents and teachers need to model these skills through their behavior and teach them directly. Setting up and using good organizational systems will hold the child in good stead in whatever endeavors he undertakes, so his efforts should be recognized and praised.

4. The child who is disorganized and whose work, materials, appearance, or room is messy is not necessarily willfully defying demands to behave differently. He may not be able to organize effec-

tively unless he is taught carefully to do so. Just as the poor speller needs consistent, frequent direct instruction in an atmosphere of respect, so too does the child who lacks organizational skills.

5. As a practical demonstration of the positive value of developing organizational skills, one of the most important and satisfying experiences parents and teachers can provide for a student is giving him the opportunity to teach another student or family member a system he has devised, practiced, or perfected.

Getting Organized on Paper

Here are some suggestions for helping children who have specific difficulties with the visual-spatial skills needed for paper-and-pencil tasks:

1. Specially lined paper is available for a variety of purposes. Since visual-spatial organization affects meaning in math (place value is determined by the location of numbers in columns), using large (½-inch) graph paper helps students set up math problems so they can read and solve them easily. Similarly, young children can use wide-ruled paper with guidelines to practice letter formations, and older students find that two-column notebook paper helps them to organize information. (See page 189 for an illustration.) Organization, not neatness, should be the focus of attention. When students achieve good organizational skills, their work generally improves in appearance as well.

2. We should not expect students to understand how we want them to set up a paper for writing without instruction and practice. In every class, there are students who need step-by-step directions for setting up margins, placing headings, spacing text, and related writing skills. Particularly if their writing has been limited largely to "fill-in-the-blanks" worksheets, they are unlikely to be familiar with accepted formats for organizing written work.

3. A technique that decreases visual confusions when students are writing and editing is having the students write on every other line. Then they can edit what they have written, filling in correct spellings and word choices in the space directly above the writing they have done.

4. Computers are among the best and most satisfying tools for students who have trouble putting their work on paper. Fortunately, most students enjoy working with computers and accept the discipline they impose. Through self-guided exploration and direct instruction, students can practice organizing text and varying layout, thus developing an eye for what works.

Interpreting Visual Aids, Charts, and Diagrams

Many secondary school and college courses rely heavily on information and concepts that are visual in nature. Mathematics, especially geometry, and laboratory and computer sciences are examples of courses that are likely to present information and concepts in varying visual formats. Among the many visual references that students at higher levels must be able to understand and remember are charts, diagrams, and graphs.

Remembering the slogan "A picture is worth a thousand words," parents and teachers may assume that these visual aids are self-explanatory. For students with strong visual skills, they are, but for those less visually adept, they are likely to be confusing. The ideal time to establish a base of understanding the components of charts and graphs is when they are first introduced in elementary school. With a good foundation and with continued explanation and discussion, most students can become proficient in interpreting information presented in this largely nonverbal manner.

Older students who lack skill in interpreting visuals can make up for lost time if teachers, tutors, or parents are willing to meet them at their level of understanding, no matter how elementary, and provide them with the base they are lacking.

1. Language paves the way to understanding visual representations. A teacher might explain, "This is a flow chart, where each box represents a step in a process. Each branching line shows a choice that can be made."

2. Analogies that use familiar examples from everyday life—from cutting pizzas into wedges to driving on branching highways—are particularly powerful tools for understanding visual aids. To check and develop students' understanding, have them explain the visual representation clearly in their own words and then teach others what they know. Preparing their own charts and diagrams for various purposes (scheduling, planning) and explaining what

they are learning will strengthen their ability to make sense of these materials.

3. Activities at home that involve building models, assembling puzzles, playing board games, and reading maps all help students to understand visual representations.

CONCLUSION

We have covered a wide range of school tasks and visual learning skills in this chapter. If your child has difficulties with these skills and tasks, the first step is having a thorough eye examination to see whether there are any structural or disease-related causes of poor vision. The examination will also determine whether vision is adequate for typical school tasks, such as reading and writing and copying from the board. It's important to note that visual acuity often is *not* the problem when a child is having trouble learning from what he sees.

Many parents worry when their children have trouble discriminating, orienting, and remembering letters and words. Fortunately, many excellent techniques exist for addressing these difficulties. Research supports the view that the sooner the child receives help, the better. Most children who receive instruction that meets their needs and whose language skills are age-appropriate go on to become good readers. If the child continues to make frequent discrimination or reversal errors in second and third grade, particularly if his difficulties are accompanied by delays in language development and academic progress, parents should consider having him tested.

It is normal for students to make mistakes when

trying to understand visual information or concepts or to need help understanding or organizing the vast array of information that reaches them through their eyes. These are skills that continue to develop throughout schooling. But if students have significant or persistent difficulty understanding visuals, learning mathematical concepts, and organizing space and materials, we recommend consulting with the child's teachers regarding the need for special help or testing.

SEEING: A DISCOVERY CHANNEL

Many students discover very early in their lives how much they can learn by using their eyes. Even those who aren't particularly gifted with spatial-relations talent or artistic ability may learn with enjoyment and ease when they use visual materials. While the words and sounds that they hear vanish, what they see can stay in front of them as a reference, clarifying and provoking thought.

The world is an exciting place for those who truly enjoy visual learning. The learner who observes, discriminates, categorizes, and remembers what his eyes take in establishes a storehouse of visual information and understanding. This, in turn, helps him to learn, understand, and think in nonverbal ways. As his store of visual understanding increases, he may be able to picture many things in his mind.

There are students who are able to remember visual diagrams, charts, and graphs as pictures in their minds. Some may be able to call up visual images to aid their understanding of new information and concepts; others may create such images as memory aids.

Those who can "preview"—who can visualize and analyze what they are going to do and how they are going to do it—often anticipate and avoid pitfalls. Their thoughts provide a kind of guided path that they can follow as they perform a task. Some nonverbal thinkers find innovative ways to solve problems using their understanding of spatial relations, of the interrelationships of parts and wholes, and of mechanical functions. People who can imagine and then transform images mentally are often effective and creative problem solvers.

The ability to make analogies and to see patterns—to make comparisons and connections between seemingly different objects, events, or concepts—leads some to make discoveries and to produce original thoughts. This is particularly true when they work across the traditional academic boundaries, seeing relationships among the disciplines and using these relationships to build new patterns and concepts.

Students with these abilities often bring a unique perspective to academic, professional, and personal tasks that involve comprehending, planning, and evaluating.

Brian Press, for example, describes himself as "more of a visual thinker than a verbal thinker." Combining guidance from his teachers with his own imagination, he has found ways of studying and completing assignments that work well for him.

I draw pictures to help me remember things. If I have to remember information about a certain king, for example, I draw an image, like a crown, and then connect it to icons that represent the important events in his reign. Then it is easy for me to recall the whole picture later, when I need to use the information.

He goes on to describe how he relies on his visual strengths when he has to write a story for his English class.

> I had to write a story for my Creative Writing class. I had a lot of impressions, but I didn't see how they would piece together to make a story. So I decided to use the storyboard technique from my video class to map it out. I pictured each scene. Then I drew lines between each and wrote out the transitions between them. This storyboard became the model for my story outline.

Michael King draws mental images, rather than the physical ones Brian describes. He says,

> I see patterns that lots of people don't see in things like tiles, even on the floors of bathrooms. I used to think I was stupid, but now I know that I think differently. I think in terms of a screenplay. I have to picture everything in my head from beginning to end before I start to write. If someone comes in while I'm still visualizing, I say, "Come back later when I'm typing it." When I sit down to write, the work is almost all done.

Peter Ozarowski is another college student who enjoys expressing his ideas visually—in his case, using video techniques. "I see things that aren't usually seen," he says. "I use video to help others see these things, letting the camera define what they see and present a particular point of view."

Peter capitalizes on his sensitivity to and enjoyment of color to improve comprehension when he is reading difficult material.

> I highlight using different colors. First, when I'm scanning, I use orange. Orange is for material that shows the purpose, the overall point of what I'm reading. When I'm reading, green is for the main ideas. Anything in green usually is followed by some yellow, which is the color for important examples of that idea. Blue is for new vocabulary words. The definitions are in pink. If I get interrupted, I just review where I was from my highlighting. This technique helps me so much in my hardest subjects. It's working!

Leslie Hill, a Landmark College instructor, observes that using visuals helps teachers as well as students to think and organize information. She comments, "I put all my lesson plans into a flow chart, using boxes, circles, and numbers to represent the material I want to cover and the way in which I want to cover it. I use a separate sheet for each section, so I can see all the information before me. Then I literally manipulate it to experiment with the sequence and the methods of presentation I want to use in class." She uses storyboards, Legos, Cuisenaire rods, building blocks—whatever objects are available—to help students to visualize events, characters, and concepts. "It is amazing what students can produce if you ask them to draw a simple picture to represent information they have just heard in a way that will enable them to remember it tomorrow."

Learning from What We Hear

The eyes take in and transmit visual information to the brain, where it is unified into a single piece of information. In similar fashion, the ears provide us with information that we hear. When the ears transmit sound messages to the brain, we hear a single discernible sound that we can locate in space. The eyes and ears work together, allowing the infant to identify the source of sounds, to relate what he hears with what he sees, and to make visual-auditory associations. Perceiving, identifying, sorting, and associating sounds are basic to all language learning.

Infants with normal hearing are immersed in a world of sound. Many of these sounds are non-linguistic—Kris's barking, Dad's footsteps, Sis slamming the door, or Pete crying. Each of these sounds has meaning, which the infant discovers as he is repeatedly exposed to them. Even before he understands the words "Here comes Kris," he knows that Kris is about to come into view when he hears the sound of her paws padding down the hallway.

Most important for our discussion, however, are the language sounds the baby hears. An infant born or adopted in infancy into most modern cultures, except the deaf community, finds himself in a society where language sounds are the primary means of communication. Using the neurological "wiring" that allows them to register what they hear and a brain that has an innate capacity to learn language, most children learn to speak and understand the language of their culture without any direct instruction.

Language learning depends on several sophisticated tasks. Although few children or adults are aware of these tasks and the words used to describe them, all people who learn to speak and understand language master these language components:

1. **Phonology:** the sound structure of words;
2. **Semantics:** the meanings of words and the networks of meaning among them;
3. **Syntax:** the way words are strung together to communicate ideas; the sequential patterns of sentence construction;
4. **Discourse:** the structure of stories, explanations, descriptions, and other verbal constructions longer than sentences; and
5. **Pragmatics:** the variations in the use of language according to context and purpose.

For anyone who has struggled to learn these elements consciously when studying a foreign language, the infant's ability to learn his own language simply by listening to and using it seems truly amazing.

LEARNING LANGUAGE

Learning About Language Sounds (Phonology)

In much the same way that the infant learns from what he sees, he begins to recognize the "shapes" and "movements" of sounds across the sound spectrum and to hear the silences, or "spaces," between words or sounds. He begins to identify the distinctive features of these language sounds, unconsciously developing a "filing" system for those groups of sounds that can all be considered "the same" and those sounds that are contrasted and are therefore considered "different."

He may hear the word *Mom* spoken in a variety of ways, each with its own intonation, pitch, volume, and accent. Yet, whether the baby hears the word voiced in Dad's baritone, Sis's cry, or Mom's own soothing tones, he soon considers all such presentations of the word as the same. He develops a kind of "template" for recognizing sounds that fit the same general shape in the sound spectrum and that, therefore, should be considered the same. As the baby begins to make sounds—first by babbling and later by speaking words—he reinforces this sound-sorting process.

Before his first birthday, the developing child has developed a sound "filing system," which allows him to recognize and distinguish among the sounds of his language and culture. When he begins to talk, he will speak in the accent of the culture on which his sound filing system is based.

The child's activities listening to and saying sounds and words provide the foundation for understanding the **phonology**, or sound structure, of his language. In these ways, he learns to distinguish sounds consistently and reliably, strengthening his powers of **auditory discrimination**. He is also learning to combine or blend sounds in different sequences as he talks. Children continue to build "phonological awareness" throughout childhood as they listen and speak, in activities such as rhyming, reciting poetry, speaking "pig latin," and even imitating the way others talk.

Learning About Words and Their Meanings (Semantics)

Most sounds have meaning. The sound of the car's motor may signal the departure of a visitor. The cat's purring communicates her content and comfort. When Kris growls, look out! The child discovers the meanings of these sounds by observation and by making associations. Such nonverbal sounds convey the same meaning to children in widely different cultures.

Most languages contain a handful of words that capture the direct connection between sound and meaning. "Cock-a-doodle-doo" in English, "quiquiriquí" in Spanish, and "cocorico" in French all stand for and imitate the sound a rooster makes. But most words exhibit no direct connection between sound and meaning. The child must learn the relationship between language sounds and their meanings as they occur in the language of his culture.

Before they begin to speak, most children develop a "listening vocabulary" of words they understand. By associating what they see with what they hear, they learn names and words for people, places, objects, actions, and characteristics. Most families respond to the child with delight when he speaks his first word. Parents and older siblings celebrate and share in the excitement represented by the baby's entrance into their culture of shared meaning and communication. Years later, families are more likely to remember the child's first spoken word than the first sounds he uttered or the first syllable he babbled. Baby's first word demonstrates his understanding that a sound can stand for something.

While the first words and their meanings initially

have a direct one-to-one correspondence, the infant soon starts to "network" these words with other words that relate to them in some fashion. He may associate *moon* with such words as *night, sky, bedtime, circle, ball,* and *the man in the moon.* This network of meaningful connections is called **semantics.** Depending on the family's patterns of communication, as well as on the child's ability to remember and associate words, he will develop either a simple and direct or a more richly networked pattern of language associations.

Morphemes

The first units of meaning most children learn are words. **Morpheme** is the term used to name a unit of meaning. A word such as *moon* is a single morpheme. Some words contain more than one morpheme. The simplest examples of these are compound words, such as *bedroom,* which consist of two separate morphemes (*bed* and *room*). The two meanings combine to produce a new meaning.

Small, Power-Packed Morphemes

As his experience with language grows and he becomes more discriminating in relating sounds and meanings, the child discovers there are some units of meaning that are not words but parts of words. These word parts are also called morphemes. They include affixes (letters or syllables added to the beginning or ending of words), like *-s* and *-es,* which form plurals, *-ed,* which changes the time, or tense, or verbs, and prefixes, such as *un-,* which totally transform meaning.

cat/cats   stop/stopped   tie/untie
dog/dogs   sort/sorted   dress/undress

As they hear such word pairs repeatedly, children discover how powerful these small morphemes are. They are "mere" word parts, but they alter the entire meaning of a word. Without conscious awareness of how sophisticated their understanding is, children know that the word *dogs* combines two units of meaning: (1) an animal like Kris and (2) more than one. They recognize that *undress* combines "the opposite of" and "put clothes on."

Observations like these lead them to discover the rules and patterns of language and to apply them to new words. Because not all English words follow these rules, young children often misapply them, their correct perception of the meaning and use of morphemes leading them to make logical and sometimes amusing errors. Pete, heartbroken about his smashed toy truck, commands his mother to "unbreak it." In response to his six-year-old brother's challenge "I'm bigger than you!," Pete climbs on a chair and retorts, "*No*, I'm biggerer than you!" While these uses are incorrect, the fact that children make this kind of mistake indicates that they are not merely repeating what they hear but are actually discovering the rules for using language.

Combining Words to Express Ideas (Syntax)

Once the developing child begins to speak, the day when he will combine words is near. In the "one-word" stage, the child attaches names or labels to what he sees and hears. Advancing to two words, he can modify, describe, categorize, and denote.

big dog (size)	my dog (ownership)
this dog (denotation)	two dogs (number)

As he discovers the rules for combining words, the child opens himself to the limitless possibilities for creative expression that language provides. He also begins to organize and classify the world around him in more detail.

Finally, the young child strings words together to form phrases and sentences. In English, unlike some other languages, meaning is embedded in the sequence or order of the words in a sentence. Changing the word order often alters the meaning dramatically. "The dog bit the postman" tells a very different story from "The postman bit the dog." Hearing and using sentences like "Daddy hugs Pete," the child acquires language patterns for expressing his thoughts. His first sentences generally are limited to simple subjects and actions. Later he will use connecting words *(and, but, or)* as he produces compound and complex sentences. The way words are put together to form phrases *(a big dog, on the bus)* and sentences (*He has a big dog. We rode on the bus.*) is called **syntax.**

Discourse

Once the child learns words and can put them together in sentences, he is at the threshold of enormous growth in communication skills. He will soon be able to put together several sentences related in meaning. He can then carry on a conversation, enjoy a simple story, and listen to and give explanations. By these means, he becomes able to follow and to produce **discourse,** the meaningful sequence of an increasing number of sentences.

Pragmatics: Picking Up Nonverbal Cues

As we listen to and derive meaning from the order of words we hear, we are also affected by qualities we commonly think about in relation to music: tempo (speed), pitch (how high or low), timbre (tone of voice), volume (how loud or soft), and the rhythmic and melodic patterns of the words as they go together. Our culture assigns meanings to these qualities to give oral communication a range of subtlety in expression. The sequence of words "I wouldn't do that if I were you," takes on different meanings depending on the way it is delivered and the body language of the speaker. It could convey helpful advice, or it could be a thinly veiled threat.

Nonverbal cues accompany the sequence of words we hear and provide additional information to help us to interpret the speaker's meaning. The context of spoken words also influences our understanding. People with good social skills know how to read situations and use language appropriate to the context, while those who lack these skills may miss the point in a conversation or a joke, or misinterpret or respond inappropriately to what they hear. The complex of skills that involves integrating verbal and nonverbal language to determine meaning is called **pragmatics.**

SOME IMPORTANT ASPECTS OF LANGUAGE LEARNING

Speed of Processing

Listening and learning through the ears differs in one important way from seeing and learning through the eyes. The child who relies on his visual system for information usually can look at an image as long as he wishes. The listener, on the other hand, has no control over the rate at which the sequence of sounds reaches his ears. Almost instantaneously, he must decode the stream of sound, with its many variations and changes in meaning. He may be quite limited in the time he has to absorb and determine the meaning of what he hears.

Remembering What We Hear

To be an effective language learner, the child must be able to remember what he hears. If he can hold in his mind the words he has just heard, he can examine and evaluate them much as he would an object he can see or touch. This ability is a valuable tool for language learning. It supports his ability to think about what he has heard, puzzle out the meaning of words, and increasingly as he gets older, categorize information and commit it to memory in an organized fashion.

PROMOTING LANGUAGE IN THE EARLY YEARS

The caregivers children have in infancy and early childhood are their first teachers. Whether parents, day-care workers, or full-time caregivers in the home, these people can support the child's growing understanding of language in many ways. If their speech is clear and unrushed, if they pronounce words carefully, and if they look at the child when speaking to him, they are helping the child to learn language and, at the same time, are serving as good models for speaking.

Good language modeling has limited value unless the child and the caregiver enjoy a positive relationship. We cannot emphasize too much how important for language development it is for the child to talk and interact with others. Caregivers who are good listeners and who are genuinely interested in the child and what he has to say make a major contribution to this process. They ask good questions and encourage the child to express his thoughts and feelings. They help him remember and talk about events in the past and wonder about the future. They understand that the child needs many chances to talk. By giving him adequate time to talk and by listening carefully to what he says, they set the stage for language to flourish.

In busy households and day-care centers, caregivers and family members may be tempted to speak for the child, to anticipate his needs, or to interpret his body language or behavior. Those who understand what an enormous amount of practice the child needs to become proficient in speaking make special efforts to see that he gets practice speaking for himself and expressing his needs.

One of the best ways for caregivers to promote language growth is by reading with the child. Even if the parent is limited to reading ten minutes before bedtime, establishing this habit can foster the child's appreciation for language. When the child listens to a story, he is exposed to language and usages he seldom hears in as complete a fashion in daily conversation. He learns new words in context (semantics), hears models for sentences (syntax), and becomes familiar with stories, explanations, and descriptions (discourse). Illustrations in children's books help to engage the child's attention and encourage conversation. The physical closeness and warmth that sharing a book creates also makes for stronger family relationships.

If an infant or young child suffers from frequent ear infections, colds, or allergies, he may temporarily or chronically be unable to distinguish among similar sounds, or he may fail to hear sounds in certain registers at all. Repeated incidents of impaired hearing during preschool years are a common cause for delay in mastering language. Some children suffer so much pain with early childhood ear problems that they associate listening with hurting for some time afterward. Inadequately treated ear infections can, in some cases, cause permanent hearing loss, as well as other serious problems. Children should receive prompt medical attention for these problems.

Parents, especially those whose time with their children is limited, should make special efforts to see that they have daily exposure to these critical language experiences:

1. Language that names and describes characteristics and uses of objects;
2. Language that accompanies actions taking place around the child and explains why and how those actions occur;
3. Language that goes beyond the present to describe happenings in the past or to anticipate the future by discussing what happened yesterday and what will happen tomorrow;
4. Language that develops simple stories by telling who, what, where, when, why, and how;
5. Language that asks questions; describes people, places, and events; expresses feelings or points of view; explains how to do something; or gives reasons for actions and decisions.

LISTENING, LANGUAGE, AND SCHOOL

Language is the most important tool that the child brings to school to support learning. He uses language to participate in all aspects of school life: understanding and remembering information, asking questions, making friends, socializing, following directions, asking for help, and solving problems. Language skills form the basis for mastering all the skills necessary for learning: reading, spelling, writing, comprehension, and study skills. The language skills that children master by listening and talking before they enter school are the foundation for school learning. School introduces some important changes and demands.

Learning the Language Code

The most important challenge of early schooling is learning to read, spell, and write. Young children who learn to read and spell well master the "code" of language. With or without direct instruction, they learn the letter names and their sounds (called "sound-symbol relationships") and how letters can be combined in patterns to spell words. Children who have a good understanding of phonology (the sound structure of language) are able to learn this language code readily. The student who has good auditory discrimination skills will avoid confusing words that sound almost alike (*pen/pin, caught/cot, then/than*) by recognizing the subtle sound differences that distinguish them. The child who can blend a series of sounds into a word will often become a good reader, one who can "sound out" an unfamiliar word. The child who can hear the sequence of sounds in words and represent them symbolically in that order will often become a good speller, one who does not have to rely solely on memory when writing words. Discriminating, combining, and sequencing sounds are all considered "phonological processing" skills. Most students with strengths in these areas learn to read and spell well in the early school years. Children who have difficulty with phonological processing may develop early reading and spelling difficulties.

New Ways of Using Language

Since much schoolwork involves using symbols in paper-and-pencil tasks, children entering school have to learn to understand and use language in new ways. Some words, especially directional words, take on new meanings when they are used with written assignments. The child who is instructed to put his name on the *top* of the paper and the page number on the *bottom* must learn that the teacher means

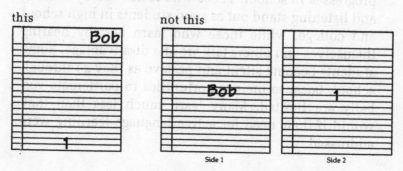

this   not this

Side 1   Side 2

We read letters and numbers from left to right. Symbols that come *before* or *after* others are located to their *left* or *right*. Numbers that are *larger* than others are greater in value, not in size of print. Words like *all together* and *equal* have different meanings, depending on whether they are being used in mathematics or history, for example.

Mastering new and particular uses of language is a challenge that continues throughout the school years and beyond. This is especially true in subjects like mathematics (especially algebra), where there is not only a specialized vocabulary but also a specialized "grammar" that is used in word problems.

Less Talking, More Listening and Reading

As students move through the grades, they have fewer and fewer chances to talk. They have to rely more and more on listening and reading in order to learn. Time for asking questions, explaining, or discussing information becomes increasingly limited. Typically, except perhaps in a few courses with small enrollments, there are fewer opportunities to "learn by talking" as a child progresses in school. Those who learn well by reading and listening stand out as good students in high school and college, while those who learn best by hearing themselves and others talk are at a disadvantage. Some students become silent and passive as they go through school, because their opportunities to participate verbally are limited. Many learn much less than they would if their need for active language learning were addressed.

Remembering Verbal Information

As students go through school, classes become teacher-centered, and students must rely more and more on their immediate memory for verbal information—the ability to remember what has just been stated. Students whose verbal memory is good, especially when it is supported by skills like note taking, tend to pick up new information, vocabulary, and names quickly. They remember information, directions, and assignments long enough to record them in their notes. They hear an unfamiliar word and remember it long enough to assign it a meaning they have pulled from the context. If something the teacher says does not make sense to them, they remember it long enough to ask for clarification. On the other hand, students who do not have a good memory for verbal information often forget information before they have even had a chance to register its meaning.

The Increasing Language Load

Most parents and teachers are aware of the increasing load of homework, the increasing difficulty of classwork, and the increasing time demands as their children move from grade to grade. Not as many are aware of the "language load" in school and how it, too, increases over the years.

Teachers talk more rapidly and use more complex vocabulary (semantics) in more complicated sentences (syntax). They speak for longer periods of time for different purposes (explaining, comparing, narrating), using different forms of discourse. When they give directions or design test questions, they use complicated constructions ("all but one of the following statements are not true") and many meaning-packed words and morphemes ("if," "however," "as soon as," "pre-read," "rewrite"). Reading assignments also increase in difficulty in similar ways. In addition, students are expected to write and speak with increasing sophistication. This "invisible" language load grows greatly as students progress through school. In order to "carry" the load successfully, students' mastery of language must keep pace with the demand.

Often, secondary schools do not teach language skills directly. Instead, the curriculum focuses on the content or information in the sciences, history, arts, English, and mathematics courses that are required for graduation. Some students can learn language skills with little direct teaching; many others need to have these skills taught explicitly.

LANGUAGE AND LISTENING PROBLEMS: WAYS TO HELP

The student who has learned how to read, spell, and write, who has developed a solid foundation of vocabulary, who knows how to understand and construct sentences to express thoughts precisely, who can recognize and use various forms of expression is well prepared for continuing education and success in the workforce. But the student who has difficulty learning language and the skills that depend on it will have fewer tools for building a solid education and constructing a meaningful life if he is not taught these skills in a way that enables him to learn them.

The most important first step that a parent can take when a child has trouble with language and listening is to arrange for a full assessment of his language skills. If he has difficulty discriminating sounds and pronouncing words correctly, he should also have a hearing evaluation. A speech-and-language therapist can be very helpful in guiding parents to decide what kinds of evaluation their child should receive. Most schools now offer evaluations to children as young as three years old and follow up with speech and language therapy when it is needed.

Although the earlier such problems are diagnosed, the better, it is never too late to seek help for language problems.

No matter how old students are, they should consider the potential benefits of testing if they exhibit persistent or significant difficulty in one or more of the following:

- pronouncing words or learning the meanings of new words
- remembering or following directions
- recalling the right words to express what they want to say
- expressing their ideas in an organized way
- remembering names and other verbal information
- comprehending what they hear or read

While many children receive help today in the preschool years, some discover much later, in high school or college, that their learning struggles are based in the areas of receiving and processing what they hear. This discovery often helps them to make sense of the past and encourages them to work on ways to compensate for their weaknesses.

Teachers and specialists are critical to addressing speech and language problems and the academic difficulties they cause. Teachers and parents can support language development in a number of ways:

1. Enhance the message.

   - Look at the child (student, or class) so he can see your mouth, facial expressions, and gestures as you talk.
   - Pronounce words clearly and with sufficient volume.
   - Speak at an unrushed pace. Use natural pauses to divide the material into phrases, sentences, and logical "chunks."
   - Reduce background noise as much as possible.
   - Support what you are saying with a picture, a diagram, a demonstration, or other multisensory materials.
   - Encourage the student to do his part—have him sit far away from the talkers in the back row and the door to the noisy hallway.

2. Make the "language load" lighter.

   - Organize what you are saying—begin with an introduction and end with a summary.
   - Say things simply first and then elaborate.
   - Introduce and explain new vocabulary before you use it.
   - Use linguistic cues ("however," "next," "as a result") to highlight the logical structure of what you're saying.
   - Allow the child enough time to process what he hears. For many students, rate of presentation is the single most important factor in determining language load.
   - Stop at checkpoints along the way to allow for questions.

- Be willing to repeat, paraphrase, or summarize what you've said, especially with information that must be understood precisely (e.g., directions, assignments).
- Ask the student to give an oral summary of important information.

3. Model good listening and speaking skills.

- Listen actively by paying attention, maintaining eye contact, and expressing genuine interest.
- Solicit your child's opinions, and ask openended questions that will encourage conversation.
- Listen patiently, giving the student time to think before responding.
- Don't interrupt, anticipate responses, finish what the child is saying, or speak for him.
- Encourage the student to express his thoughts completely.
- Avoid calling attention to mistakes or making numerous corrections. These have the effect of reducing the fluency and amount of speech, decreasing the child's confidence, and reducing his perception of himself as a valued participant.
- Start and end conversations appropriately.

4. Encourage activities that give the student an opportunity to develop language by talking, listening, and participating.

- Make time for the child to talk to a relative, older brother, neighbor, or senior citizen (or explore opportunities through Big Brother/ Big Sister or mentoring programs).

- Have the child participate in clubs, youth groups, 4-H, Boy or Girl Scouts, or other organizations that have small groups to promote participation and interaction.
- Develop times of the day when more extended conversations take place at home—at the dinner table or before bedtime, for example.
- Discuss stories, movies, and TV programs; local, regional, and national events and issues; and family activities.
- Involve the child in solving problems by having him follow directions or instructions for activities around the house.
- Tell jokes based on multiple meanings of words, or read together from a joke book.
- Develop opportunities for the child to teach or explain something to others, to share an interest, or to read or tell stories to younger children.
- Read stories, books, or poetry aloud together regularly.
- Seek activities that promote language, such as participating in a play or puppet show, or fundraising for Little League or for a class trip.
- Have the child take speech-communication or drama classes that provide the opportunity to be in a play, practice job or college interviews, or recite a section of a famous speech.

What About a Foreign Language?

Students who have trouble distinguishing, processing, and remembering sounds and words are likely to find learning a second language difficult. Generally it is a good idea to give them enough time to master the first language before they attempt the second.

They are more likely to be able to handle a foreign language when instruction takes their learning differences into account. In some colleges, teachers using multisensory techniques and giving students lots of oral practice have had notable success with these students. Such programs reinforce students' understanding of their first language by relating it to the concepts and structures in the second.

There are students who have such persistent difficulty learning language that waiving the foreign-language requirement or substituting another requirement may be justified in high school or college.

LANGUAGE USERS

We all know children who love to figure out how to take apart and put together objects in the material world. They build space stations and castles with Legos, design and construct complicated model railway systems, or draw up and use plans for building a tree house. This passion for building has its counterpart in children who are fascinated with the construction and use of language. These children delight in experimenting with and manipulating language and in exploring the infinite diversity of sounds, shades of meaning, and variations in structure. They are sensitive to the art of language, and they enjoy reading and writing, and listening to or reciting literature of all kinds.

But even those who are not gifted with language recognize its power as a tool. We use language to understand, explain, persuade, support, or oppose. When we are confused, we apply our knowledge of language as we ask for and receive help or think through the issue. When we are locked in disagreement, we call on language to mediate.

Language gives us the means to classify and retrieve memories. Using language, we can organize the past and plan for the future. We also use language when we think through projects and problems, anticipate obstacles, propose solutions, and plan for tomorrow. Language provides the means for monitoring what we are doing and evaluating what we have done.

Language is a springboard to self-expression and a pathway to self-understanding. It empowers us to become our own teachers. Using an inner voice to guide us through learning, remembering, and critiquing, we do not simply understand, but we understand whether or not we understand.

Teachers and parents who love language and who want their students and children to share in its gifts work to give students a similar understanding. MacLean Gander, Landmark College English Department chair, says:

> Landmark students have great potential to learn language skills, but they have not had a chance to fulfill that potential. They arrive with a lot to say but without the skills to do so. Developing oral and written skills with these students is like unlocking a door. Effective oral and written language skills allow students to learn in every class.

Joyce Klucken, Speech Communications chair, stresses understanding language as the basis for language learning.

The first step is learning about language. If students understand something, then they can begin to think about it. A big part of the speech-communication curriculum is the demystification of language. They learn about the concepts of linguistics: phonology, morphology, syntax, semantics, and pragmatics. As they develop an understanding of the structures and functions of language, they become increasingly aware of other people's language and their own. Developing an understanding of language is the first step because then they begin to recognize and identify what they are listening to.

She advocates for all students an active oral language program, including preparing and giving speeches, self-evaluation through videotaping, and peer evaluation based on specific goals, such as fluency, expression, and the use of transition words. She says:

> We see that as students improve their oral language, their written language improves as well. They begin to think of oral language in terms of composition. It has a beginning, a middle, and an end. It has a purpose with parts (sentences and paragraphs) that contribute to it. In addition, as students participate in speech communication classes as peer evaluators, their listening skills improve dramatically.

Andrew Feinberg, a former Landmark College student, describes his experiences:

> I was shy. I remember being told in class, "You have good ideas," but I thought just the opposite. My speech communication class helped me branch out and take

risks. Now I believe I have ideas that are worth sharing because I know how to express them.

I'm also more sensitive to the way people express themselves—the emphasis they put on certain ideas because of the words they use. I'm a lot more conscious of what people are saying, how they are saying it, and when they aren't using words correctly.

Now, when I speak and write, I'm always looking for more active words. When I get things wrong, I know how to find my mistakes. I've gotten better at taking constructive criticism.

Often, when I am writing, I will brainstorm out loud, to make sure I get all my ideas into words. I read my papers out loud to find my mistakes. I even study out loud, by myself or with a study group. Talking helps me get my ideas out, clarify my understanding, and remember what I am learning.

Learning by Doing

Some people learn best by actually performing those tasks that require them to use their hands and eyes. In the computer exercise on pages 23–24, all but the first three options depend on learning by doing.

I'm a hands-on learner. When I was a kid, I excelled at hunting, fishing, target shooting . . . anything I could get my hands on. After high school I went to work for a heavy construction company. I was the best heavy-equipment operator, and I got a certificate in welding.

Jack

George, now a college student, relies on learning by doing. Listen to his description of how he approaches his work.

If I can sit and see how the pieces fit together, I can understand and remember. Watching someone doing a task and then mimicking what he does is a good way for me to learn. I learned from my father, by following him around and then trying to do what he was doing. This is how I learned how to do everything from mowing the lawn to installing a stereo system, by watching and helping and then doing it by myself. I would never have learned if he had sat me down and said, "Now I'm going to tell you how to install a car stereo system or mow the lawn."

We tend to first think of "motor" or "muscle" skills in relation to athletics and the performing arts. We admire professional athletes and reward the best of them handsomely. Corporate leaders choose sports events or the golf course as the places to go to make deals. High school athletes have very high status in the adolescent world and bask in a culture of appreciation and support provided by cheerleaders, pep rallies, and publicity. We also recognize the fine motor dexterity of the skilled surgeon and the gifted musician. Yet we seldom think about motor skills in relation to conventional learning.

But motor skills are as important in the classroom as they are on the athletic field, on stage, in the operating room, or in the working world. In school we rely on our motor systems to communicate everything that we see, hear, read, think, imagine, or wonder. Academic

assignments usually involve our fine motor system—
the ability to use the fingers to convey thought by writing or typing and the mouth to talk and express ideas.
We call on our gross motor systems when assignments
involve building models or presenting demonstrations.
Every expression of what we think or know involves
some part of our motor system.

Our motor system allows us to do more than simply
express what we know. It also provides a way for us to
be intimately involved as we are learning. For many
people, "doing" is critical to the process of learning
itself. "Doing" promotes learning.

DEVELOPMENT OF MOTOR SKILLS

The infant learns by doing from the day he is born. No
one has to teach him to use his hands together with the
muscles of his mouth to nurse. Nursing is one example
of a coordinated chain of movements called "reflexes"
the infant is able to perform. Most children are born
with a "motor program," which allows them to carry out
this and other actions necessary for survival in infancy.

As infants grow, they learn to control the voluntary
movement of their bodies, though at first in a very im-
precise way. Some of their earliest movements are gross
motor movements that engage the whole body—
kicking, flailing their arms, arching their backs, or roll-
ing their heads.

Several processes are at work in developing the
motor system. With time, movements such as nursing
become more voluntary, more versatile, and less "pro-
grammed." In addition, the baby's gross, or whole-body,
movements are becoming more precise or refined. He

turns only his head, rather than his whole body, toward the door when Dad walks in. When he reaches for a toy, he moves only his arms, hands, and fingers.

Before long the infant begins to develop fine motor skills, the ability to use the "distant" parts of his body, especially his hands and fingers, in refined and precise ways. Soon he can pick up a particular Cheerio with just two fingers and place it in his mouth. Movements not only become more precise, they also become more energy-efficient, as the infant begins to inhibit extraneous movements. The baby who has been using both arms to reach and pick up his rattle now uses only the arm closest to it. His other arm rests quietly at his side.

From the beginning, the child is networking motor movements with other developing learning channels. The infant looks as he reaches, using feedback from his eyes to guide his fingers. The continuous feedback provided by his eyes helps his fine motor control become more precise. Later, he will walk along the street with his father, and pick up a toy he has dropped, using information provided by seeing to tell him how far to walk and how far to extend his hand to pick up the ball. He will incorporate his father's linguistic cues into his actions ("Be careful and stay on the sidewalk").

As he develops, the young child becomes able to put together increasingly longer chains of movements. A sequence of movements becomes fluid, or smooth, and then increasingly rapid. Finally, the sequence of motor actions is performed accurately, efficiently, smoothly, quickly, and without a lot of attention. It is seamlessly networked with other functions—looking, talking, listening—which help to guide performance. We say that such actions have become "automatic."

Whether we are watching an athlete playing on a

ball field, or a fourth-grader writing on the chalkboard, we can assess the quality of their motor performance in terms of these factors:

- efficiency (how much extraneous movement or effort is apparent)
- precision (how accurate or precise the movements are)
- fluidity (how smooth the sequence of actions is)
- speed (how quickly the actions are performed)
- networking (how effectively they work with other functions)
- automatization (how much conscious effort or attention is required to perform the action)

MOTOR MEMORY AND PLANNING

There are a few other functions that relate to using the motor system fully as a channel for learning. The first is **motor memory**—the ability to remember and learn what we have just done. For many students, practice that involves body actions is the most effective way to learn and remember such things as letter formations, the spelling of words, multistep procedures in math, formulas and their applications, and scientific concepts and procedures. Students whose motor memories are strong have a remarkable tool for learning in school. They literally remember the "feel" of things they have learned.

The second is **motor planning**—the ability to think about what we want to do and to translate our thoughts into a sequence of actions. For some students, this is an effortless process. They may decide to catch a ball, take homework out of a book bag, or write a cursive capital letter with little conscious attention. Such students find it easy to combine and recombine small actions into the smoothly connected sequences of actions required for accomplishing larger goals.

USING THE MOTOR SYSTEM IN SCHOOL

Sitting Still

When children enter school, they discover that certain motor skills and behaviors are highly valued. For example, they learn that teachers place great importance on students' ability to sit still for extended periods of time. It may seem odd to begin talking about "motor" skills that are valued in school by first talking about "sitting still," but children often quickly come to believe that being "good" means sitting still, without talking, and giving the appearance of listening attentively to the teacher. This is the message many teachers (and parents, as well) send, whether directly or by inference.

Careful listening, thinking, and performance all involve mental activity. Some students find it easier to concentrate if they engage in motor actions, such as chewing gum, cracking their knuckles, or jiggling their legs. "My engine idles fast," one student declared. Parents and teachers may find these actions distracting, annoying, or even confrontational. For these students the effort to keep their bodies still, while paying active attention with their minds, can be exhausting.

Gross Motor Coordination

Starting in early childhood, a young person's self-esteem is often strongly molded by his ability to throw, catch, kick, and run in individual events or team sports. A student with poor gross motor skills, even if he is at the top of his class academically, may be embarrassed and feel isolated when he is the last one chosen for teams, when he is teased for being clumsy, or when he is blamed when his team loses. Students who are awkward in their movements or clumsy in handling materials are at risk for developing low self-esteem.

Fine Motor and Graphomotor Skills

Starting in the earliest years of school—in preschool and kindergarten—there is a great demand for development of fine motor skills as the child engages in activities such as cutting, coloring, buttoning, tying shoes, and drawing. In kindergarten and first grade, children begin to receive instruction in learning to print and write, perhaps the most difficult fine motor tasks children must learn. There is a separate name for these skills—"graphomotor" skills. Every young student spends substantial time developing them.

Variations in how quickly children develop fine motor and graphomotor control are to be expected. Young writers with fine motor problems who grip the pencil tightly in order to control letter formations often feel discomfort and tension in their hands and arms, and sometimes in their neck, jaw, and even their back and upper body.

Many preschoolers and kindergartners who appear

clumsy in their handling of materials go on to develop smooth and efficient handwriting. But a graphomotor problem can quickly turn into a difficulty with spelling or with writing compositions if the child's needs for practice and appropriate teaching are not addressed.

Visual-Motor Skills

Visual-motor (eye-hand) skills also make an important contribution to success in schoolwork. Not only must the child see the difference between r and n, his hands must also be able to reproduce the letters accurately enough so that others see them as two distinct letters. The biology student must be able to draw clear representations of what he has seen in the microscope. When copying from the chalkboard or other visual displays, the student has to reproduce with his hands the directions, notes, symbols, and other information the eyes have seen before the visual is changed or the board erased.

Speed and Fluency

As children proceed in school, they meet greater demands for rapid and automatic fine motor performance in writing and keyboarding. Starting in the middle school years, students have to think about the content of their composition at the same time they are writing or keyboarding. If they also have to think about letter formations, legibility, spacing, or keyboarding, they cannot perform higher-level thinking tasks easily. Efficient note taking, composing, and other study skills depend on well-developed fine motor skills.

HELPING STUDENTS WITH GROSS MOTOR PROBLEMS

We tend to think of athletic ability, or "gross motor coordination," as an innate ability that a person either has or does not have. In fact, motor skills develop over time, and the rate at which people acquire these skills varies enormously. Many children continue to improve their coordination significantly throughout adolescence, some improving dramatically as they use their thinking and language skills to conceptualize motor skills and promote coordination.

Recommendations

1. Competitive sports can place children in a pressured environment. For those students whose motor coordination is poor, this pressure can be particularly troublesome. Parents can play a key role in counteracting the atmosphere that surrounds competitive sports by encouraging activities that promote fun, risk taking, teamwork, and individual development. These students may enjoy sports and activities such as swimming, running, weight training, bicycling, gymnastics, dancing, horseback riding, and skiing.
2. Certain sports (such as baseball, volleyball, and tennis) and certain positions (goalkeeper) require precise eye-hand coordination and timing, in addition to other gross motor skills. These sports and positions may be intimidating for students with visual-motor coordination diffi-

culties. Such students may prefer ball sports where the ball does not routinely approach the face (such as soccer) or participation in the athletic activities listed in the first paragraph.

3. Activities like karate, rock climbing, and orienteering promote coordination by actively engaging the mind as well as the body. These may be attractive to students who enjoy a thinking, problem-solving approach to activities.

4. A student whose passion for a particular sport is not matched by athletic ability may enjoy filling an alternative role that respects his interests and abilities. Having him serve as a scorekeeper, announcer, reporter, or manager are positive ways for him to participate in these activities.

5. Students with more significant motor-development delays may benefit from participating in adaptive physical education classes, where activities specifically address deficient motor skills.

Helping Students with Fine Motor or Graphomotor Difficulties

Michael, who thinks creatively but has difficulty with fine motor skills, describes his hands as the "exit ramp" for the ideas on his brain's highway. "It's like having potholes on the exit ramp and your ideas getting caught in a traffic jam or even a crash as they try to get off."

Those with fine motor and handwriting problems are often embarrassed because it takes them so long to complete written assignments, even when they find the content easy to understand. They may feel ashamed of what they produce on paper, knowing that others will judge it to be careless or messy. They may also be angry that they are being judged on the appearance of their work, rather than on its content. Sometimes they are frustrated because even they cannot read what they have written.

Children and adults with these problems may find themselves cut off from the personal satisfaction and positive feedback that comes from admiring and sharing finished products with others. The mental and physical attention and effort the student must give to the task of writing may interfere with other tasks that must be performed simultaneously, such as letter formation, spelling, sentence structure, and organization of ideas. His written work may include many errors in areas the student feels he knows well.

Recommendations

1. Even in the world of the word processor and the laptop computer, it is important that students practice and become as fluent as possible in handwriting.
2. Students who feel tension or pain in their hands, fingers, or bodies often are unaware of changes they can make to relieve this. Teachers can help by demonstrating how to hold books and place paper comfortably in relation to the eyes and the body. They can teach students how to use their bodies to maintain an alert, tension-free position when they read, write, work at the computer, and perform other fine motor tasks. They can help students develop a comfortable, relaxed pencil grip, and show those who need additional help how to use a plastic pencil gripper to train their fingers to the cor-

rect position. In the past, many naturally left-handed children were required to learn to write with their right hand. Today most educators agree that the student's natural preference for hand use should be respected and encouraged. Left-handed children need special guidance from teachers to establish the hand and body positions and paper orientation that produce comfortable writing conditions. Some students need time and gradually increasing amounts of practice to replace old habits with these new ones.

3. Although it requires a little extra effort, guiding students to collect appropriate tools and materials for writing pays off. Even those students who dislike writing often enjoy figuring out what materials work best for them.

- Students at all stages of development do better work when they use paper that provides ample space for writing. Students with graphomotor difficulties should avoid narrowly ruled paper, which is likely to create problems with note taking, editing, and legibility. When selecting assignment notebooks, calendars, and other organizers, they should check to see how much writing space is provided.
- Students who break pencil tips as they try to balance the demands of pressure and control in writing should carry a good supply of pencils and a pocket sharpener in their book bag or notebook. Soft pencil-top erasers are a must for the student who has to make many corrections.
- Students who need to feel where their fingers are as they write usually prefer felt-tipped

pens to ballpoint pens, which provide little friction and therefore give little feedback to students. Some students find pens with thicker shafts more comfortable to hold than the traditionally sized pens or pencils.

4. Whether children should learn and use print or cursive letter formations exclusively, or learn both systems, is a source of continuing controversy. While there is no single correct answer for all children, there are some general guidelines. Students often have a strong preference, which can be the deciding factor.

Cursive Writing

- If the child has a strong motor memory, cursive may be a good choice. Cursive formations have the advantage of reinforcing spelling by creating a feel (or motor memory) for common sequences of letters *(ght, ould, tion)*, for common word patterns, and for words as a whole.
- Similarly, a student who has difficulty remembering the orientation of printed letters may prefer cursive formations because they are practiced as single, whole movements. He may compensate for his poor visual memory for symbols by using his stronger motor memory for cursive formations.
- Cursive writing is generally an excellent choice for children who are good at motor planning— producing chains of motor actions with little apparent attention. These students frequently develop fluid handwriting, a tremendous strength in upper levels of schooling, where they need to take notes and write quickly.

- Many students who have initial difficulty with cursive formations find it helpful to practice large formations on the chalkboard, trace on a rough surface, and write on wide-ruled paper with guidelines.

Printed Letter Formations
- Other students are more comfortable and efficient when they stick with printed letters. These formations require students to master a limited number of motor movements, which are assembled in parts to produce a letter formation.
- For students who tire during fine motor activities and who have difficulty chaining motor actions, printed formations have advantages. These students may find printing less tiring, more comfortable, more automatic, and faster.
- Students who have trouble mastering symbols may find their printing easier to read than their cursive writing. For them, printing is desirable because they can access their own written work more readily.

5. For all people, but especially for those with poor graphomotor skills, the computer is one of the best lifelong tools. When they first begin to use computers, some students have difficulty learning keyboarding and word-processing skills and may require individual or self-paced instruction. If they are also poor spellers, it will take more time for them to learn to keyboard. Imagine what it would be like if you had to learn to type using another language with unfamiliar spelling patterns! Most of us would rely on "hunt and

peck," typing letter by letter, until we learned the letter patterns and mastered the spelling of words.

6. Each child has his own rate of moving and working. Some will never complete assignments in the time considered reasonable for their peers. Most, however, can improve the pace of production when the motor issues discussed above are addressed and when they are given practice in writing and keyboarding. Even as they practice and improve their writing skills, they may still require some accommodations such as a reduction in the amount of copying they must do, or extra time to complete written tests, to copy notes from the board, or to produce a drawing in lab.

7. Students with weak graphomotor skills often find writing so frustrating and tiring that they learn to hate composition assignments, even though they have good ideas and creative imaginations. They need opportunities to compose without writing, perhaps producing a speech or a tape or dictating a report to a family member or friend. Such activities minimize production problems and can give students greater interest in composition. Unhurried discussions at home and in school provide opportunities for explanations, narratives, storytelling, and debate, all of which support the process of composition.

8. To counteract the discouragement they feel when their written work is returned covered with corrections, students need opportunities to produce writing that is not subject to correcting. Examples of ways to practice writing for fluency and coherence are journal writing, diaries, and

correspondence with a friend or relative. With correspondence, if the person receiving the letters keeps them filed by date, the student can review them in the future to evaluate his progress.

Students whose fine or gross motor-coordination difficulties are a significant or persistent source of embarrassment, frustration, or interference in their daily activities may benefit from having their skills assessed by a physical or occupational therapist for more specific recommendations.

The Motor Learner

Some parents and teachers seem to consider education as exclusively a matter of the mind, giving physical and hands-on education a lower status. When a student's grades are poor, he often has to give up athletics, the arts, or an after-school job, these being viewed as less important than academic subjects. High school students who "can't make it" academically may be directed to more "hands-on" courses of study. Athletes receive applause for their achievements on the playing field, but unless they are also good students, they may be sneered at as "dumb jocks." A student who knows how to use his body as a way of learning and expressing himself, however, has a remarkable and versatile resource for lifelong learning.

By using their bodies to express and interpret what they see, students may display their talent in comedy, dance, mime, and drama. The athlete and the dancer use their bodies to express power and grace, as well as to project a physical presence. Students who are strong motor learners may struggle in school but thrive in the workforce, which provides varied opportunities for on-the-job training. There are many ways for them to use their talents in school as well, however.

Linda Hecker, Landmark's director of Tutorial Services, and Karen Klein, of Brandeis University, have developed several exciting programs that capitalize on the motor strengths of students. One of these they call "walking essays."

Starting with one main idea, the student demonstrates physically how ideas and details in the essay relate to one another. If a detail elaborates on the idea he is working with, he takes one step to the side to indicate that there is a link between the detail and the idea. If a new idea is introduced, the student shows this by taking a step forward, and if an idea or detail contradicts the one being discussed, he takes a step backward.

According to Linda, this exercise fosters language development for students who learn best by doing. As students move forward, backward, and to the side, they verbalize the reasons for their actions and often have to defend these reasons to their classmates. They may add words such as "however," "although," "as a result," and "in summary." These are linguistic markers that contribute to the flow in writing and make the argument or explanation clearer to the reader.

Another innovative method for developing language involves the use of Tinker Toys and Legos to construct models of the material being studied. One student, Linda tells us, was struggling to organize an essay on the role of China in world politics. Her tutor gave her a set of Tinkertoy and said, "Forget about words for now. Just show me how the ideas fit together." After the student built the model, she described it, and told what idea each piece represented and how these ideas were connected. Following this exercise, the student was able to use her three-dimensional model as a guide for preparing an outline for the essay she had been assigned to write.

Once teachers and students begin to explore alternative ways of handling assignments, they usually discover that there are countless methods for approaching each task. Being freed from conforming to models that rely almost exclusively on learning by seeing and by hearing, students often surprise themselves and others with their insights and abilities.

Kristin Lougheed, a former Landmark College student, did an independent study entitled "Movement and Academics: The Bridge to Success." In her paper, she explores the uses of bodily intelligence in the study process. Kristin comments,

> I want to break down the conception that we have to sit still to learn. I know that I need to incorporate movement into learning. It breaks down the physical monotony of learning and encourages me to be involved in what I am learning.

Kristin is a dancer—she enjoys movement and activity and has a remarkable memory for things she has done. She uses her talents as a bridge to the academic world of studying and organizing. She has used whole-body movements to reinforce spelling patterns and vocabulary words and definitions. She organizes her classwork and homework in space, and she creates concepts like a time line, which she can move and talk her way through. Kristin doesn't limit her creative ideas simply to movement, however. She writes, talks, and uses visuals as well.

> The combining of all the ways of learning—listening, seeing, moving, everything combined together—is what makes the most potent learning experience of all.
>
> Kristin

3. Memory, Attention, and Automatization

With a background in the ways we can learn from what we see, hear, and do, and with an understanding of language as the primary tool for learning in school, we turn now to examine three functions—memory, attention, and automatization—which determine how well we make use of the information we receive. We will use a simple analogy in this chapter—comparing information processing in the brain to the workings of a busy office. Although the analogy is not scientific, it will help us to clarify these important and complex learning functions.

Memory

> I thought when I got to high school that learning would involve more thinking, and in a few classes it did. But mostly it was just a lot more memorizing. I always felt like a camel carrying one too many straws of information.
>
> Steven

Central to all forms and types of learning is memory. What we remember and what we forget, how we remember or forget, how memory is tied to our ability to receive and store information, and the role of memory in understanding and relating information are all crucial parts of the learning process. Our storehouse of memories contains the record of all that we have experienced and learned. The process of forgetting is our way of uncluttering the storehouse. Our abilities to remember and to forget influence who we are and how we approach the world.

REMEMBERING AND FORGETTING

We all remember many of the things that we want to remember. These things may be as practical and routine as remembering the bus schedule or the name of the boss's son. They may be unusual or striking experiences, ranging from the joyous feelings and images surrounding the birth of a child to a particularly hilarious scene in a movie. We remember, with little or no effort, how to perform certain actions, like swimming or riding a bicycle, even years after our most recent swim or ride.

We also remember many things we'd just as soon forget. Some of these are trivia we have no use or feeling for: the phone number of a house we lived in many years ago, for example. Others may be those events and emotions that have played a part in shaping who we are—the pain of broken relationships, of disappointments—those images that erupt uninvited and cause us to relive unhappy experiences.

On the other hand, we all forget many things we want to forget—the identification code for a bank card we no longer use, names and faces of casual acquaintances, people from our pasts whom we are unlikely ever to see again.

But for most of us, and especially for students, the major memory problem is forgetting what we want to remember. We recognize a person who speaks to us, but we cannot think of her name. We take a test at school and can't remember the formula that we knew so well last night. We practice and learn a list of twenty new spelling words but only recall half of them correctly on Friday's weekly test. We answer a question about a movie or book we've really enjoyed and discover that we can't remember details essential to the discussion.

REMEMBERING WITHOUT EFFORT

Before we take a detailed look at the memory demands of schooling, let's examine our ability to remember things without consciously trying to do so. This will help to identify factors that we can use to help us remember the things we have to learn intentionally.

There are countless images, actions, and pieces of information that fill our environment. We "sponge up" some of this information spontaneously and, without conscious effort, store it in our memories. However, the kind of information we remember spontaneously, even about the same event, will vary, depending on the sensitivities, interests, and background knowledge of each individual and on the nature of the stimulus received.

WAYS MEMORIES DIFFER

If we ask members of a family what they recall about their last Thanksgiving reunion, we are likely to discover that their memories vary widely. Food, people, conversations, football games, time shared between a child and an adult—family members will recall some things clearly and others little or not at all. Consider these sounds, tastes, feelings, scents, and activities from a typical family Thanksgiving:

- Aunt Mimi's stylish clothing, sweet smell, and warm laugh;
- the turning point in a football player's career based on his memorable performance in a game;
- the smell and taste of Aunt Joan's raspberry pie;
- Aunt Mimi's description of her trip to Africa;
- playing "pound the pan" with Uncle Jim;
- learning how to program a computer with Uncle Howard;
- the dinner table conversation about the recent election.

Discovering the kinds of information we spontaneously or easily absorb helps us understand what our strong learning channels are. It indicates whether we are especially sensitive to information coming through our eyes, our ears, our actions, or a combination of senses. It gives us clues to the kinds of environments in which each of us is likely to learn best. Some of us learn and remember best from rapid-paced discussions and debates, others from quiet contemplation of visually stimulating surroundings, still others by engaging in hands-on activities.

MEMORY AND UNDERSTANDING

We also learn easily when we are learning new information that is related to what we already know. It fits readily into our existing network of information. Aunt Joan, who neither understands computers nor wants to, doesn't remember Uncle Howard's discussion with Peter. But for Peter, who enjoys using computers, that discussion remains his strongest memory of last Thanksgiving. He not only recalls most of what Uncle Howard taught him, he even found a mistake his uncle made in presenting the information.

When we have a background of vocabulary, knowledge, and interest in a particular topic or subject, as Peter has for the computer, our memories are more receptive to additional information on the topic. This relationship between understanding and memory provides one of the strongest means for remembering what we want to remember.

BIG IMPRESSIONS ARE LASTING ONES

We also tend to remember more easily experiences that are registered strongly. Memories of exciting, unusual, or emotion-filled events fall into this category. Few of us will ever forget the TV images of the tragic bombing in Oklahoma City. Older readers can describe in detail where they were and what they were doing when they heard about the assassination of John Kennedy. You may have vivid memories of a championship game, of

the night you saw the northern lights, or of an embar-
rassing experience in school.

But we also retain more routine information when
it is registered strongly. We may know what to buy at the
grocery store even though we left the list at home because we remember the act of writing the list. We remember a speech we gave several years ago because we
rehearsed it out loud repeatedly, but we may have little
memory for one we read from a text. We may recall in
detail one battle of the Civil War because we participated in a historical reenactment of it, but perhaps we
cannot remember much else we read about it in the
American history textbook. We know the phone number for a hardware store in the town we used to live in
because we dialed the number so many times when
building a house ten years ago. The strong impact of
such experiences ensures them a place in memory. If we
study how a memory can be made stronger—for example, by verbal rehearsal, by writing, by participation, or
by repetition—we may gain some insights that will help
us improve our memory for material we must deliberately learn.

In each of these examples, we remember information because it has been repeated frequently or because
we have processed it in more than one way. By these
means, we have increased the *depth of processing* (we
have registered the information more strongly), and in
so doing, have fixed the information in memory.

PASSION FEEDS MEMORY

When we care passionately about something—music,
art, literature, major-league sports—we are likely to re-

member, almost without conscious effort, new ideas, information, and content relating to that area. The intensity of our feeling for the subject acts both as a magnet, pulling the material into the brain, and as a glue, adhering it firmly in memory.

HOW WE REMEMBER: A SUMMARY

There are several key factors that influence the extent to which memory contributes to learning:

1. the nature of our most sensitive learning channels;
2. the power of background knowledge and understanding to improve our memory for new information;
3. the learning techniques that help us to register information strongly (increase the depth of processing);
4. the roles (i.e., magnet and glue) that feelings and interests play in registering information strongly.

PROMOTING MEMORY: WHAT TEACHERS AND PARENTS CAN DO TO HELP

I always felt that my brain was like a closet crammed with files that teachers had just chucked in and then slammed the door.

Rob

Students with memory problems, especially younger students, are tremendously dependent on "good teaching" in order to learn. Although there are many variations, there are principles of teaching that promote memory.

Those who communicate with students by using several "learning channels" reach many more types of learners in and out of the classroom than those who rely on one channel only. Many students can learn when only one channel, such as looking or listening, is required. But others, those who are not particularly strong in one channel, understand and retain information better when they receive it through more than one. We have seen the value of engaging each person's learning strengths in the earlier chapters. To review, here are some creative ways to help children use their strong learning channels.

- Use clear and well-designed visual references and aids, such as pictures, charts, diagrams, graphs, and models presented on the chalkboard, overhead projector, computer screen, or handouts.
- Speak clearly at an unrushed pace with adequate volume; minimize distracting background noise and adapt your presentation to the vocabulary and conceptual ability of the audience.
- Encourage students to participate in thoughtful discussions by speaking, summarizing, explaining, elaborating, drawing analogies, evaluating, and expressing personal reactions.
- Provide opportunities to "learn by doing," whether in the biology lab or in Dad's workshop; to role-play; or to go on field trips that have been

planned purposefully and are followed up with activities, discussions, and assignments.

When teachers and parents use multisensory teaching techniques, or call on many "learning channels," as described above, there are combined benefits. These techniques also increase the depth of processing, by registering information strongly through several different channels. A student is far more likely to remember something that he has read about, discussed, written about, and/or participated actively in than something he has simply read.

Because people remember more easily when they are learning material that is related to what they already know, parents and teachers can capitalize on the relationship between memory and understanding by presenting new information in a way that emphasizes the logical structure of the material to be remembered. The following suggestions will help parents and teachers support each student's ability to remember what he understands.

- Start with an introduction that develops the purpose of the lesson or activity, and conclude with a summary of what was accomplished.
- Use linguistic markers—those words and phrases (such as "first," "next," "as a result," "in summary," "the main idea") that point out the temporal, spatial, or logical relationships between ideas.
- Avoid "rote memory" exercises whenever possible, where names, dates, and other information are simply memorized.
- Help students discover the context and back-

ground for the material being learned, and embed facts and details that must be memorized in a "web" of understanding.

- Design classwork that encourages cumulative understanding, summary, synthesis, and comparison.

Parents, advisers, and older siblings can help students who lack background knowledge in the content of some subjects by pointing out the value of taking introductory courses and by serving as study partners who listen as the student rehearses and explains the content and concepts they are studying.

Students remember best when they learn from teachers, parents, or coaches who are passionate about what they do, who share their love for their subject, and who inspire in others the desire to learn. Their joy can be the spark that ignites an area of interest in students, thus strengthening the memory processes. Students are inspired by teachers who communicate not only their love of the material but also their love of the process of learning.

REMEMBERING OVER DIFFERENT PERIODS OF TIME

We take in and remember some information just long enough to use it and then we discard it by forgetting. Other information sticks with us longer. Educators and psychologists have identified several types of memory, which we will discuss by comparing the way we handle information to the way in which an office receives, stores, retrieves, and evaluates (saves or discards) information.

Recognition Memory

Picture a telephone operator, receptionist, or secretary—that person in an office whose job involves "reception" of the diverse information that reaches the office. The telephone rings. It's Ms. Sanford. She identifies herself as a publicity and marketing specialist. The "reception-ist" recognizes her name because she has called before. He attaches her name to a preexisting memory. Although he could not have recalled her name if he had been asked before her call, he remembers now that she called several times last week trying to reach the boss. This kind of memory, which involves recognizing but not recalling, is called **recognition memory**. Ms. Sanford wants to schedule an appointment with the boss next Tuesday at 3:00 P.M. She needs directions to get to the office, and she chats briefly about the recent snowstorm.

Short-Term Memory

Without trying to record the entire conversation verbatim, the "reception-ist" then makes a temporary record of the information on a message pad. He reduces it to preserve the essential information: the name of the caller and the date, time, place, and purpose of the appointment she wants to schedule.

Neither Ms. Sanford nor her message is part of the company's permanent records at this point. There is only a "short-term" record (**short-term memory**) of the information. Subsequent experience will determine whether and how any information about Ms. Sanford will be filed and used (remembered) or discarded (forgotten).

The "reception-ist" has done a good job with this short-term memory task because the message was simple and clear, and because he has developed several important skills:

- He understands and processes language quickly;
- He attends to the message and ignores distractions;
- He differentiates between important and unimportant information;
- He organizes, summarizes and reduces the information; and
- He employs strategies such as note taking and repeating information, to check for accuracy and completeness.

Long-Term Memory

If the boss decides that Ms. Sanford and her services will be useful and important and that she is the person most able to provide marketing services, then, in a well-run office, a "Sanford" file will be created. (This is comparable to a person's **long-term memory**.) Material such as proposals, brochures, samples, plans, and minutes of meetings will be retained in this permanent file as long as Ms. Sanford continues to work with the office staff.

To ensure the efficiency of the permanent files in an office like this, there are several considerations.

1. The files must be categorized clearly;
2. They must be well organized within and among categories;

3. The files must be networked with related preexisting files;
4. The files must be regularly used and updated.

Active Working Memory

While working on the marketing plan, Sanford and the office staff may take some materials temporarily out of related long-term folders and place them, together with more recent short-term materials, into a special folder designed for this project. They will file all materials relevant to the project here. This special folder is comparable to a person's **active working memory**. When the project is complete, materials will either be refiled in the permanent files (long-term memory) or discarded. An efficient project file depends on these factors.

1. All files relevant to the task are assembled;
2. All files are complete; and
3. All files can be easily and simultaneously accessed.

TYPES OF MEMORIES: A SUMMARY

Recognition memory involves realizing whether information is new or whether we have encountered it previously. When we say, "I can't give you directions, but I'll recognize the turns as we get to them," we are relying on recognition memory.

Short-term memory allows us to record and remember information for a very short period of time after it is presented. Short-term memory serves as a "waiting room" through which all information passes before entering the large "long-term memory" storage area. For most people, short-term memory is limited in capacity, usually to seven or fewer items. For this reason, telephone numbers, excluding the area code, contain only seven numbers, and for the same reason the waiter reciting the list of the day's specials may lose his customers' attention and ability to take in information if he offers a lengthy listing of its ingredients, sauces, and side dishes.

Long-term memory is the "permanent storage area" for our memories. Here we store the words, information, ideas, facts, and procedures that together make up our own personal knowledge. The capacity of this storage system is almost limitless, but its efficiency depends on how well the filing system is organized.

Active working memory is the "work area" at the forefront of our consciousness where we collect the information we are thinking about and where we use it to solve problems. We call on working memory when we solve a mathematical word problem, simultaneously remembering math facts and processes, specific conditions presented in the problem, number formations, and the vocabulary that directs us to the steps required to solve the problem.

MEMORY AND SCHOOL

Parents and teachers often talk about the workload that students have and whether it is a reasonable expectation for a particular grade or student. In addition to this workload, students also carry a "memory load" of information they need to retrieve to complete classwork and homework. That memory load can be extensive, as is

illustrated by a list of information that elementary
school students typically are expected to memorize.

Letter names, sounds, and formations
Alphabet
Days of the week
Months of the year
The spelling of words
Math facts
States and capitals
Oceans, continents, countries
Vocabulary words and their definitions
Rules of capitalization and punctuation
Telling time
Regrouping in calculations
Arithmetic processes (adding, subtracting, multi-
plying, dividing)

Children who are creative, original thinkers often
are bored or frustrated by the amount of memorizing
required in the primary grades. If they have trouble
memorizing material that others find it easy to file away,
these children and their parents and teachers may conclude that they are lacking in intelligence, motivation,
or potential. There is a danger that these negative conclusions, made when children are young, can become
self-fulfilling prophecies. In the section on automatization, which follows on pages 127–136, we provide additional suggestions for helping elementary school
students in this area.

The quantity of memory tasks increases and their nature changes as students enter secondary school and college. The number of long-range assignments increases, as does the interval between tests. Students need to develop better ways for retaining and retrieving information over longer periods of time. Here are other factors that affect the "memory load" of high school and college students:

1. Information is less likely to be presented in the multisensory manner described earlier. Instead, students are expected to get most information by listening to lectures and reading textbooks.
2. Little if any direct instruction in the skills that support memory is given at these levels. Students are expected to select, categorize, retrieve, and relate information with minimal help from teachers.
3. Active working memory is subject to especially heavy demands. Students have to listen, take notes, integrate information from other sources, paraphrase, and categorize almost simultaneously. Assignments often contain information that students must relate to prior knowledge. Simultaneously, they must recall related facts and processes and put all of these pieces of information together to produce a good answer. Students whose long-term memories are weak or whose recall of basic information is not automatic are likely to need considerably longer than the average amount of time to perform simultaneous thinking and remembering tasks.

SOME COMMON PROBLEMS WITH MEMORY AND SOME WAYS TO HELP

Short-Term Memory Difficulties

Some children forget, either fully or partially, information they have just taken in, sometimes only seconds after they receive it. Like writing in sand at the beach, which is erased when the next wave washes over it, the stimulus or piece of information is lost. The memory process is short-circuited at its very beginning. Children with short-term memory problems may gain little from the incidental learning that most people acquire simply by experiencing events as they happen, whether or not they are focusing their attention on what is happening.

Memory problems are often related to a variety of other learning difficulties. Children with attention problems may not attend to the information they must learn, they may not be able to identify what it is important to remember, or they may not use memory strategies. Children with language-processing problems may have similar difficulties, or may simply not understand what they are hearing as it is being presented. Some children have trouble with short-term memory in one particular learning channel.

- Students with poor short-term visual memory who are unable to organize and remember what they see in chunks may look back and forth from the board or projection screen to their paper as they attempt to copy information.
- Students who have problems with short-term au-

ditory memory may signal this by continually asking, "What?," by repeating or whispering the information to themselves, or by relying more heavily on visual clues.

- Students with limited memory for a sequence of actions may have difficulty repeating a dance step, a basketball shot, or a letter formation they have just learned.

Fortunately for those who have problems in this area, there are many academic skills and memory techniques they can learn to use.

- Calling on strong learning channels and increasing depth of processing, as discussed earlier in this chapter, are good methods for students with short-term memory difficulties.
- Because short-term memory has limited capacity, students must be able to recognize what information is important and what is not. Most students profit from direct instruction and practice in distinguishing main ideas and details, important and unimportant information, and relevant and irrelevant information.
- Students also need direct instruction in those academic skills that support short-term memory, such as note taking, abbreviating, paraphrasing, summarizing, and organizing or "chunking" information.
- Students need to be taught and given time to practice how to set up and keep calendars, assignment notebooks, and similar planning and record-keeping devices that reduce the memory load they must carry.

The amount of information each of us receives far exceeds the capacity of our short-term memory. Successful executives and successful people with learning differences—often the same people—demonstrate similar organizational skills and habits. Once they have put a system in place and use it as a habit, they experience few difficulties.

Problems with Long-Term Memory

Long-term memory is a storage system that depends on the ability to organize (file away information according to topic) and to interconnect (put together related information) material. Some students develop efficient "filing systems" with little or no guidance, while others need direct instruction and practice before they can organize and "record" incoming information so that it can be retrieved easily at a later date from long-term memory.

Most long-term memories are stored in categories. The first step in retrieving information stored in long-term memory is thinking about categories of information. Because memory is closely related to understanding, remembering often involves reconstructing information based on that understanding. People with good long-term memories are usually conscious of the way they store information. Those with long-term memory problems seldom categorize information, either at the time they acquire it or when they later remember and reconstruct it. Just like the office workers described earlier, some students can locate and remember information easily, while others can't find in memory information that they "know" and need.

Students who have difficulty with long-term retention of information should learn and apply a study system such as the Master Notebook, described in Chapter 6. Few students learn these study skills independently, but most students can master them with direct instruction. Most good study systems advise students to follow these steps:

1. Listen for key words and phrases ("as a result," "therefore") and look for other information (boldface headings, titles) that gives clues about the structure and patterns of the material under study. Identify the main ideas and the important details.
2. Understand the key concepts, the vocabulary words, and the structure and principles of the information. Discover the relationships among different pieces of information. Organize the important information into logical groups, or "chunks" which can be remembered as a whole.
3. Practice and study information using your own sensitive learning channels. For example, if you learn well by seeing, make a diagram to clarify your understanding or develop a time line for a history course.
4. Register the information strongly (increase the depth of processing) by practicing it as many ways as possible. Use pictures, charts, and diagrams; write summaries; engage in question-and-answer sessions with a study partner; rewrite your notes; or recite information out loud.
5. Talk, explain, and repeat the information out loud. This technique—called verbal rehearsal—is one of the most effective ways to promote long-term memory.

6. Make the information more meaningful by relating it to your interests and by developing analogies. Compare and contrast the information with other material you know well.

7. Practice summarizing the information (reducing it to include just the main points) and then elaborating on the information (expand and explain ideas using important details and examples).

8. Practice information even after you understand it. This promotes more efficient, accurate, and complete recall of information.

9. Study in shorter, more frequent study sessions, and avoid cramming, all-nighters, and other marathon study sessions.

MEMORIZATION

Unfortunately, students have to learn many things, especially in the early grades, that do not naturally fall into a framework of meaningful organization. For example, there is no logical reason for the order of the letters in the alphabet. In addition, much of what they need to file in memory consists of material that holds no intrinsic interest but constitutes the building blocks for later, more interesting learning. The alphabet, arithmetic facts, days of the week, months of the year—knowing these is essential to understanding how language, time, and the physical world are ordered. This kind of information must simply be memorized "by rote."

The following principles and suggestions may be helpful to parents and teachers in assisting students with memorization tasks:

- Explain and circumscribe the material that must be simply memorized, so students are not under the impression that most of what they must learn in school is an arbitrary collection of unrelated facts.
- Encourage students to be active learners, even during memorization practice. Active learning can take the form of discovering and sharing memory strategies that work best. Many of the memory techniques discussed earlier in this chapter will be helpful. Learning how to memorize and use one's memory as a tool is a skill even young students can enjoy learning.
- Explain any structure or pattern in the material to be memorized. The interrelationships of math facts (e.g., 3×7 is the same as 7×3), the patterns associated with math facts (e.g., counting by 5's), and even irregular spelling words *(would/could/ should)* can be useful in helping memorization.
- Develop a mnemonic, or memory aid, to help organize and retrieve the information. For example, the word HOMES can help a student remember the Great Lakes: Huron, Ontario, Michigan, Erie, and Superior. Visual techniques, such as the one suggested by Brian in Chapter 2, can also serve as memory aids.
- Identify the particular type of memories that are hard to establish (e.g., sound/symbol associations, or memorization of strings of items such as the alphabet) and develop specific techniques to help. The section on automatization will address these issues in greater detail.

PROBLEMS WITH ACTIVE WORKING MEMORY

Many, many students have trouble with active working memory. In school, students are frequently asked to do several tasks at once. Succeeding at this kind of simultaneous processing task is addressed in detail in the section on automatization.

MORE THAN MEMORY

Teachers who present organized instruction in the skills and processes that underlie efficient memorization often discover that all students, those with learning problems and those without, become stronger, more enthusiastic learners. Long after students have forgotten the details they memorized for a particular course, they will continue to call on the skills they used to promote memory and understanding.

Parents can set the stage for their children to learn these skills by modeling some of the techniques described in this section at home. In addition, they can communicate clearly with teachers about the types of memory difficulties their children are having and help their children cope with the memory demands of school. Parents whose children experience persistent problems memorizing should consult with their teachers to see whether an evaluation of their abilities in this area would be advisable. The many ways parents can support learning at home will be discussed in more detail in Chapter 7.

Attention

"Pay attention!" We all know what that means. It's clear
and simple. It has to do with focusing and concentra-
tion. When we don't get things done the way we wanted
them to be done, it is often because we did not pay
sufficient attention. "Pay attention"—we say it to ourselves, our children, and our friends. But let's take a
closer look at some situations where we say this and see
what different shades of meaning it can have.

You're driving alone at night, exhausted after a long
day at work. Suddenly you find yourself cruising along
at 85 miles per hour. You slow down, concerned that
you might fall asleep, fail to react to approaching cars,
or drive off the road. You stop to wash your face with
cold water and drink a cup of coffee, warning yourself
as you get back behind the wheel, "Pay attention."

You are attending a lecture in a course required for
recertification in your field. Through the open doorway
to the hall, you hear people discussing the double over-
time soccer game in which your daughter scored the tie-
breaker the day before. Turning to the window, you see
several people attempting to jump-start a car by pushing
it. A classmate comes in late and takes the seat next to
you. He rummages noisily through his briefcase and
then asks you to lend him a pen. You become aware that
the professor has been lecturing for several minutes and
that you cannot recall anything he has said. "Pay attention," your internal monitor says.

You are learning a new way to figure depreciation
costs and concentrating so intensely that you do not

hear your study partner enter the room. When you go over your work with him, he points out a simple error in addition. "Pay attention," you chide yourself.

You are delayed at the office. Your son's day-care center closes in ten minutes. You have to stop at the grocery store before going home to make dinner. After dinner, you have to get to the hospital to visit your father before eight o'clock. You turn off the computer, pick up your briefcase and purse, and turn off the lights as you lock the door. Riding down on the elevator, you are caught short by a mental picture of the ring holding your house and car keys sitting on your desk. "Pay attention," you lecture yourself as you try to find the building superintendent.

When we examine situations in which we berate ourselves for not paying attention, we find that attention has a variety of meanings. Here are some common meanings we have for the phrase "pay attention":

- "Wake up. You're not alert. You're not thinking clearly."

- "You're paying attention to everything but what you need to be focused on."

- "You're so involved in your work, you are oblivious to everything that is going on around you."

- "You're making careless mistakes."

- "Your mind is not on what you are doing."

- "You don't finish what you start."

Clearly, attention includes a variety of functions that control and regulate what we think and do. Here are some of the most important of those functions.

- **selecting** what is important, and ignoring or **filtering out** what is not essential to the task at hand;

- **allocating** mental energy to specific tasks, and **shifting** focus among them;

- **previewing** what we're going to do, **monitoring** what we're doing as we do it, and **checking** what we have done; and

- **regulating** our physical and mental energy, as well as thoughts, feelings, and desires while we work.

To make the attention functions more concrete, we return to the analogy of the business office.

SELECTING AND FILTERING

Because people, like most business offices, receive far more information than they can possibly use, they must sort the information, decide what is important, and determine how much attention each piece of information deserves. In a business office these jobs are assigned to the receptionist, secretary, or mail clerk.

Picture a steady stream of messengers arriving at the central office. Some bring information in an orderly fashion (neatly organized in a briefcase), some dump piles of unrelated information (the daily sack of mail), and some discover that they have come to the wrong office and leave. The receptionist has to deal with each of these messengers, often giving as much attention, if not more, to those who have to be directed elsewhere.

Most business managers know that productivity decreases dramatically when there are problems at the initial level of selecting and sorting information. The receptionist who is distracted by visitors and by the hum of office equipment, the switchboard operator who clogs the telephone lines with personal calls, the mail clerk who misroutes messages, the secretary who is unsure of the level of importance of pieces of information, and the clerk who discards first-class mail and pores over catalogues and advertisements all have their functional counterparts in children and adults with attention problems. The difficulties they experience, however, unlike the behavior of several of the employees described above, are not under their willful control.

Students whose ability to sort information is inefficient are often described as distractible. Some have trouble identifying what is important, others have trouble filtering out the sounds and sights in their environments. Still others become so lost in their internal thoughts, distractions that are invisible to the observer, that others see them as daydreamers.

Here is how Alex Knowlton, a former Landmark College student, described his struggle to focus:

> Wandering through the flickering images of memory and thought, "What to write the paper on?" is the question that echoes through this landscape. So many things floating around in the mind to write on. Each one expanding into view, then once again shrinking down into the background when a new idea comes to mind. When

> finally I choose one, my mind sees the details clearly.
> But great is the urge to continue wandering around and
> exploring the mental landscape that surrounds and en-
> traps, with wonder, the wandering mind.

ALLOCATING ENERGY AND SHIFTING FOCUS

The language we use in discussing attention reflects
another function, allocating our mental resources. We
speak about *pay*ing attention, attention *deficits*, and
*spend*ing our energies.

Just as we are presented with more information
than we can possibly pay attention to, we also have
many more choices and possibilities for actions and
activities than we can possibly pursue. Once we have
selected what we want to do, we face the task of allocating mental energy to the task. This is true for businesses,
too, and most offices have someone who fulfills this
function—usually an office manager.

When a business undertakes a specific project—
mailing an advertisement to a target group, for example—the office manager is responsible for coordinating
the various jobs this entails. The project requires different kinds and amounts of effort at different stages.
The office manager draws up a schedule to ensure that
the various steps are completed in the appropriate
sequence—she oversees the development of the marketing plan, the writing and designing of the advertisement, and its production and dissemination. The office
manager is also responsible for seeing that the special
project does not force the shutting down of other office
activities. Workers assigned to the special project from

time to time must shift their energies back to the routine assignments they are expected to carry out.

Students who cannot develop the sequence of steps to be followed in order to reach a goal are prone to jumping from one to another or skipping some of the steps. They often appear impulsive in their manner of approaching tasks. If they do not know how to allocate and spend their energies, they may either overlook or put too much energy and effort into some steps, or they may get sidetracked into irrelevant or peripheral activities. Sometimes they become so involved in one activity or aspect of the assignment that they have trouble shifting their attention to other activities important for completing the work, or back to routine events of daily life. Or they may be so distracted by all the other things they must do that they cannot attend to the task at hand.

PREVIEWING, MONITORING, AND CHECKING

Quality control—making sure that the activity completed or product made meets a certain standard—is one of the most important functions in a business office. Quality control includes knowing the characteristics of an acceptable product, understanding how each step in producing it contributes to its quality, and knowing how changes in the process affect the outcome.

Three important skills students need in school are previewing or picturing what they are going to do and anticipating the possible results, monitoring what they are doing when they are doing it, and checking it when they are finished. Many students have problems with this. Their understanding of what they need to accomplish and the steps required to do so may be unclear or inaccurate. Or they may not have learned specific checking skills, such as using addition to check the answer in subtraction, or proofreading papers before submitting them to be read and graded. These students are often poor at self-assessment, predicting how well they performed on a test or an assignment.

REGULATION

When an office is run efficiently, we are not aware of the invisible factors that support productivity, but even a brief power failure makes us conscious of the unseen systems we rely on without thinking.

Imagine a day in an office when there is a breakdown in one or more of these systems. The automatic thermostat may be set for 70 degrees but may be poorly calibrated, so the temperature dips to a frigid 45 degrees before the furnace kicks in. Once the heat is on, it does not go off until the temperature is a stifling 95 degrees. Or the thermostat may be permanently set at too high or too low a temperature.

Or suppose the lights for the inner offices, which are on a timer, do not come on until 10:00 A.M. and then stay on until 2:00 A.M. Electric power is on during the workday, but there are irregular outages that bring work to a standstill and power surges that sometimes result in the loss of data in computers. The regulatory functions of the Central Office have their counterparts in those functions involved in arousal and alertness that support a person's ability to sustain attention and be productive.

Students whose sleep patterns include bedtime wakefulness or interrupted sleep or who resist getting up in the morning are likely to be tired and groggy during the school day. Sometimes they actually fall asleep in class. These students may be at their peak at 11:00 P.M., enjoying mentally stimulating activities like playing chess or discussing politics. Other students show no such distinct pattern, working productively in spurts but tiring or becoming bored easily. They may require excessive amounts of time to complete tasks or have chronic difficulty finishing their work. Some students have a hard time regulating or modulating their physical and mental energy, as well as their activity, feelings, desires, or interests. They have ups and downs, often being perceived as moody, reactive, erratic, restless, sluggish, or overactive.

Recommendations

1. Students who frequently exhibit behaviors like those described above should be tested to see whether they have an attention deficit hyperactivity disorder (ADHD), known popularly as attention deficit disorder (ADD). Testing will also indicate whether the presence of other conditions (e.g., seizure disorders or emotional issues) is contributing to the attention problem. Attention problems are complex and often aggravated by other conditions.

When students find it hard to concentrate and pay attention, they deserve treatment based on an understanding of their needs. The most common treatment possibilities for students diagnosed with ADHD/ADD are specialized coaching, teaching, tutoring, or counseling; modifications in their educational programs; and medication. It is essential for students whose attention problems coexist with other learning problems (memory and language processing problems, for example) to get help in those specific areas as well.

2. At the simplest level, help for students who have trouble paying attention involves enhancing the clarity and effectiveness of the message, decreasing distractions, getting organized, and increasing active involvement in learning. These recommendations involve the essential themes of this book. Specific suggestions discussed throughout the learning chapters may be appropriate for or adapted to the needs of these students.

3. Students with these problems are often subjected to name calling and labeling. Those who call names and use labels seldom realize how damaging they can be. Calling students "space cadets" or telling them they are "off the wall" defines, demeans, and isolates them. Name calling and labeling do not promote positive changes, and they distract attention from the central issue, which is for students to understand their behavior and the ways to modify it.

4. Students with attention problems tend to be more aware of their deficiencies than of their strengths, so they need special support in identifying and cultivating the latter. Parents and teachers may point out to the student who is easily distracted by internal thoughts that these thoughts often signal the presence of a creative imagination for which they should seek outlets. Channeling this creativity into the lesson or activity can turn "distractions" into "attractions."

5. Coaching—the guiding support of a teacher, parent, or other mentor—is one of the most effective ways to help a student with attention problems. Coaching is particularly useful at the beginning and end of tasks—the stages of planning the project and of reviewing and checking it when it is finished. Younger students and

those with long assignments may need coaching at intermediate points as well. Coaching should be direct and concrete, emphasizing the sequencing of skills. Few students improve when coaching consists largely of cheerleading, encouraging them to try harder without giving them concrete suggestions.

6. Parents and teachers may have to expand their own views of what constitutes acceptable studying and learning behavior to include more movement and activity. Some students need to take more frequent breaks while studying, change positions and work locations, and move about physically while thinking or studying. They can take these breaks at points in an assignment that represent completion of subsections in order to promote a sense of accomplishment.

7. In secondary schools and colleges, academic help is often provided on an "on-call" basis, where students come in at the point in the semester where they are having difficulty. Unfortunately, some students do not realize they need help until they find themselves "swamped." Such students need to develop the habit of using coaching or tutoring early and regularly during the semester.

8. Students with a history of sleeping and waking problems do not find it easy to change established patterns. They need routines that become habitual and provide reliable patterns in their lives. A healthy diet, daily exercise, and waking and sleeping routines help to establish these habits. They also need balance, however. A highly planned and rigid schedule may increase their anxiety and their attentional difficulties.

Getting children, especially teenagers, out of bed in the morning can turn into a daily battle in many households. To the extent that the age and maturity of the

126 *Carolyn Olivier and Rosemary Bowler*

child permit, parents should support them, yet give them the responsibility for this and other problems. A parent who takes on and continues the roles of the awakener, planner, organizer, reminder, and custodian of the lost-and-found department is likely to find that his child is neither independent nor grateful for his efforts.

9. Like most students, those with attention problems are able to learn and develop many more skills when they are working on a topic they enjoy. They may be able to learn and practice skills they perceive as "less interesting" (like note taking) when they are exploring and organizing information that has real meaning for them.

CONCLUSION

"You're not paying attention" is perhaps the most common observation made about children who are having trouble in school. With all the publicity surrounding the diagnosis of ADHD/ADD, it is tempting to self-diagnose, or to jump to the conclusion that attention is "what's wrong."

Difficulty paying attention may be a symptom of many other problems, however. It is also important to remember that we don't pay attention to what we can't or don't know how to do. At the same time, remember that almost all children, indeed most adults as well, behave impulsively; are distracted by competing sights, sounds, and thoughts; or find sitting still difficult from time to time. Like all human behavior, attention is subject to variation from person to person and within each person. If, however, these fluctuations are frequent and persist over time, they may indicate the presence of a problem that needs to be identified and treated.

Because attention is an important learning function, students with attentional problems are likely to need special help with school. Throughout this book—in every chapter—we suggest ways to maximize learning, no matter what the cause of the learning problem may be. Each chapter provides ideas for helping students become more efficient and productive learners. For more information about learning problems, including those that involve attention, we suggest you look into the resources listed in Appendices C, D, and E.

Automatization

No matter where we are—at home, in school, at play—we often have to handle more than one task at a time. We give little thought to the actions required to sweep the floor when, at the same time, we answer our children's questions about homework. We carry on conversation with our friends about the movie we are going to see at the same time that we calculate the cost of tickets and count our change. As we drive, we listen to the passenger reading the directions to our destination, glance at the map she puts on the dashboard, and read the highway signs.

When we do several things at once, we may give most of our attention to one task (answering questions about homework) and little attention to the other (sweeping), relying on skills and knowledge we have made nearly automatic. Or we may shift our focus back and forth between the tasks. If we have to tackle two demanding tasks at the same time, however, we find it almost impossible to give each the careful attention it requires. If we shift our focus back and forth between them, we must allocate extra time to get both tasks done. It is much easier to do two things at once if one of them can be done automatically.

Stores advertise time-set coffeemakers and telephone-answering machines as "automatic" because they require little of our attention. Similarly, information we can remember and tasks we can perform with little attention are considered to be "automatized." When information or tasks are automatized, using this information or performing these tasks becomes almost as effortless as breathing. Automatized information enables us to look up a friend's number in a telephone directory quickly, tell time at a glance, or, without thinking, hit the shift key on a typewriter or computer keyboard when we want a capital letter. We do not, when we need a capital, stop and think deliberately, "Now, I need to have a capital letter because I am starting a new sentence. To do that I must reach for the shift key, press it, and hold it down with a finger on my left hand while I press down the letter I need with a finger on my right hand."

We do not merely remember automatized information and skills. We have learned them so well that we can use them while our attention is directed elsewhere.

AUTOMATIZING A NEW TASK

To make the process of automatization more concrete, let's use the analogy of learning to drive a car. When you learned to drive, you had to think consciously of each step. "To start the car, I have to put the key in the ignition and turn it to the right. Then I put the shift into reverse, release the brake, and step on the accelerator." Your driving instructor helped you by limiting her conversation to the task at hand: "There's a stop light at the end of this block. Slow down now and prepare to put your foot on the brake and come to a complete stop. Now, look carefully in both directions before you take your foot off the brake and place it back on the accelerator."

With continued practice, you gained control of the driving process. You no longer gave conscious thought to starting the car, although you still had to think carefully when driving in traffic or at higher speeds. Eventually, you became comfortable driving because you automatized the various tasks involved. Today, you hop into your car, listen to the radio, carry on a conversation with your passengers, review the major points in the report you will be giving at your destination, and reach that destination, often with little or no recollection of the actual journey.

There is considerable variation in how well individuals can automatize certain skills. Even in a society where almost everyone drives, there are some people who choose not to do so because they find that despite practice and good instruction, they are unable to make automatic the steps and sequences that driving requires.

Experienced drivers generally concentrate much more closely on what they are doing when weather or traffic conditions are poor. They may find it difficult, perhaps impossible, to carry on a conversation, to follow verbal directions, or to review ideas. They must focus their full attention on driving. Instead of hearing the news commentator on the radio, they may hear their inner voices saying, "Maybe I should switch into four-wheel drive here," or "If I use my low beams, that should cut the glare from the snow and give me better visibility."

Anyone who has driven in a snowstorm or a tropical downpour knows how nerveracking and exhausting it can be. These feelings are like those described by a college student who was overwhelmed in a lecture class. He described feeling as if he were driving through a blizzard as he tried to take notes, select important ideas, and concentrate on the mechanical skills of writing, all at the same time.

AUTOMATIZATION IN SCHOOL

In school, students are frequently asked to perform several tasks at once. For example, good readers perform two essential processes. They translate the printed symbols on the page into the words they represent. This process is called decoding. At the same time they are decoding, they call on their general knowledge and their understanding of language to construct the meaning of what they are reading. This is the process of comprehension. Good readers decode almost effortlessly (automatically) so they can focus most of their attention on the flow of ideas and the development of meaning as they read.

Failure to automatize basic language skills is one of the most common causes of reading and writing difficulties in students of all ages. If students cannot decode automatically when they read, they have little attention to spare for comprehension. If they read slowly enough to assure accurate decoding, their comprehension may be diminished, and they may have to reread the assignment several times. Alternatively, if they focus on comprehension, they often make decoding errors that distort meaning and interfere with understanding.

Earlier we discussed the differing philosophies of teaching reading. In an effort to provide young children with greater exposure to good literature, many schools have eliminated direct instruction in decoding entirely. The student who does not readily automatize decoding may compensate in early grades when he can grasp meaning from illustrations and from familiar stories, but he is likely to suffer in the long run. In higher-level reading, the author often embeds his meaning in words unfamiliar to some readers. The reader has to decode these words accurately in order to preserve the author's meaning and to expand his own vocabulary and knowledge base.

Similarly, the writer who struggles to spell, form letters, and punctuate constantly interrupts his thinking as he switches attention from the ideas he wants to express to the mechanics he needs for expressing them. If he concentrates on mechanical accuracy, his writing seldom demonstrates how knowledgeable and thoughtful he is. If he concentrates on the ideas he wishes to express, his work may be riddled with mechanical errors. One such student described her reaction when she got back a composition she had labored over and found it covered with corrections in red ink. "It looked like my teacher popped an artery reading my paper!"

Students who can perform efficiently in a wide range of school tasks have a store of information they can access automatically (see page 107).

Students who master skills and knowledge to the point where they can use them automatically have an advantage in school. The math student who has auto-matized facts and processes can apply them efficiently and accurately when he must read and solve a problem. The student who automatically recalls the alphabet can look up information in dictionaries, telephone directo-ries, indexes, and other reference materials quickly and accurately.

Students of all ages whose decoding skills (or other language skills) are not automatic can improve them significantly by using techniques described elsewhere in this book. As they become more proficient and auto-matic in decoding and other skills, they can pay greater attention to ideas and meaning, and consequently their performance can improve in areas such as reading com-prehension, writing, note taking, and other study skills.

Recommendations

1. We all vary in the types of information and skills we can make automatic and the rate at which we do so. But when young children fall behind their classmates in basic skills—such as learning letter names, formations, and sounds; remembering word meanings; telling time; and mastering the sequence of the alphabet, the days of the week, and the months and seasons of the year—we recommend that they be tested to see whether they have dyslexia or another learning disability. Because this es-sential learning comes easily to other children, those who have difficulty often feel that they are not smart. They may lose interest in school and appear poorly motivated. Often their parents and teachers will see them in this way as well. Testing helps assure that these issues can be addressed early, before larger problems develop.

2. Unfortunately, some children who have these difficulties repeat their first-grade year without recognition on anyone's part that they need a different teaching approach. Using the same methods and materials again is likely to be as effective as prescribing a second round of an antibiotic that a sick child has not responded to simply because most children do get good results from it. The child who has not made language skills and processes automatic usually needs to be taught by different methods if he is to have success. Parents and teachers need to look carefully at recommendations regarding grade retention for the child with automatization difficulties.

3. Good initial teaching and regular, effective practice are the keys to making language skills automatic. Some children need much more practice than others, however. Parents can work in conjunction with teachers to provide regular, short, frequent practice of particular skills at home. Indeed, such practice makes ideal homework in the early grades. Students can practice using methods and materials that work best for them. They can keep records, chart their performance, celebrate their successes, and report results to their teachers.

4. Many students respond poorly to the unimaginative or overly simple worksheets that are often used for skills practice. They may be entirely correct when they call these exercises a waste of time and may react more positively when practice consists of multisensory methods that fit their particular learning needs. Parents and teachers can help them to understand that automatizing academic skills (such as reading, spelling, note taking, and math facts) depends primarily on practice by comparing them to nonacademic skills they willingly practice. Just as driving a car, serving a tennis ball,

or playing the guitar become automatic only after extended practice, handling words and numbers without
conscious thought requires a lot of practice. Some
skills, whether motor or intellectual, may never become
fully automatized, but the more we practice them, the
better we can perform.

5. Parents may be the first ones to notice that their
older child is much less efficient in completing homework assignments than his general level of understanding suggests he should be. They may observe that "he
reads the history chapter two or three times before he
understands it," "He has great ideas when he talks
about his assignment, but he loses track of what he
wants to say as he is writing," "He knew those spelling
words last night, but he doesn't know them this morning," or "He makes a lot of 'careless' errors in his written
work." These observations are clues that the student's
skills may not be sufficiently automatic to support
learning. No matter how old the student is when he, his
parents, or his teachers develop concerns about these
matters, testing to identify the nature of his learning
problem is appropriate.

Older students with these automatization difficulties become increasingly at risk as they progress
through school and as the gap between their skills and
their understanding widens. Although they may enjoy
the content of challenging courses, they may perform
increasingly poorly on tests and assignments. When
these students are tested, the examiner usually can determine what they need—specialized tutoring or
classes, for example—to develop the skills they lack.

6. Students are more likely to be willing to tackle
assignments that are difficult for them when teachers

give separate grades for content and mechanics on written work, or acknowledge correct application of mathematical processes despite calculation errors.

7. We have discussed several ways that the computer supports learning for all students. It is also useful for practicing language and learning skills. Software programs that provide skills practice, initially little more than electronic workbooks, are improving each year in interest and effectiveness. Spell checkers, calculators, and electronic dictionaries make completing assignments easier for the student who has not automatized all the skills involved in advanced academic work.

8. Performance improves when students concentrate on one skill or process at a time. One system that can help involves subdividing a task into its subskills and taking up each in turn. To proofread an essay, for example, the student might first read it focusing on the sentence structure, making sure that all sentences are complete and that the subject and verb agree. On the second reading he might check spelling and punctuation, and so forth. With this approach to proofreading, the student will see improvement in the quality and rate of his work.

Charles Drake, founder of Landmark College, was one of the first educators to see the relationship between automatization and problems that children and adults with dyslexia have in mastering the code of language. While working to develop teaching methods and materials to help these students, he also recognized the value of the mind that does not readily fall into automatic habits. He observed that many students who have trouble with automatization are creative thinkers who approach tasks and solve problems in original ways. Unlike the problems presented in learning to read, few problems in later life can be solved "automatically." They require the kinds of minds that think about what they are doing as they are doing it.

4. Interconnections and Chain Reactions

In this chapter, we show how the seed for future learning problems is planted when variations in learning are not recognized, understood, and respected.

> Students who learn differently do not get the kind of attention and instruction they need. If someone had figured out that I was truly capable of learning but marched to a different drummer, maybe I would not have had so many problems in school and then later in my relationships with people.
>
> Anna

The term "chain reaction" came into general usage in the 1940s as a result of the splitting of the atom. In atomic physics, the term is used to describe the cumulative effect of splitting atoms in nuclear fission, in which one split causes others, each of which, in turn, causes others. In similar fashion, individuals, all of whose life experiences and functioning abilities are interconnected, are subject to chain reactions. With respect to issues of learning, we need to look at the effect that interconnections and chain reactions can have on learners who encounter obstacles in school.

In the last two chapters we described what is involved in learning and what can interfere with that process. We provided some practical examples of the different ways in which we learn and discussed some of the causes of learning problems. One reason children and adults with learning problems are often misunderstood is that the process of learning is an invisible one, and teachers and parents are not always aware of the subtle signs that point to those differences in learning.

Remember Eric, in Chapter 1, who wished that his learning differences were visible? He wished others could see when and why he was struggling, could give him the help he needed, and would not misunderstand him or misjudge him. No parent or teacher would expect a child whose leg is in a cast to enter a footrace and then admonish him to "try harder" or encourage him by saying, "We know you could win this race if you really wanted to." Yet parents and teachers make such misjudgments when they do not understand the child's learning differences.

Whether a child learns best by seeing, by using language, by active learning, or by some combination of these means, how efficient his memory is, how well he can pay attention, and how efficiently he can use his prior knowledge are all factors deserving understanding and respect. When parents and teachers do not provide that understanding and respect, what may begin as an invisible difference, a variation in learning, is likely to emerge at some point in the child's life as a significant problem.

Consider Shawn, whose hands and fingers just don't seem to be able to work together quickly when he first has to produce written work in elementary school.

If his parents and teachers do not recognize this first visible sign of an invisible learning difference, what starts as an issue of motor speed and control may become a major problem when he reaches secondary school. There he will be required to produce large quantities of written material within strict time limits. If Shawn encounters frequent failure as a result of his difference, he is likely to show signs of emotional distress.

Here the chain reaction starts with poor fine motor coordination and control. The student develops poor handwriting, produces messy papers, and takes a long time to complete written assignments. Parents and teachers attribute his difficulties to inadequate effort and require him to copy his work over. When he spends additional time on his written work and his efforts do not lead to noticeable improvement, his frustration builds. Every time he picks up a pencil, he feels anxious and resentful. He writes as little as possible and frequently does not hand in written assignments. Disciplined in seventh grade by having to write a sentence over and over, he "overreacts" angrily. His behavior and grades fall steadily. By the time he reaches high school, he has established patterns of withdrawal, work avoidance, low expectations, and diminished self-esteem. None of these behaviors would have been predicted by someone who was familiar with his personality when he entered school.

Many college students and older adults recall incidents they now can recognize as the indications that they learned differently from their classmates. Most of them see that failure to understand and address such issues when they first appeared ignited the chain reaction that eventually led to much more serious problems.

Let's listen to some of these students describe how misunderstanding of different ways of learning set the stage for their later failure and frustration.

Joan, a college graduate and now a teacher, still recalls hearing, over and over, from the time she started school, "Come on, Joan. Just pay attention, listen, and follow directions. Stop daydreaming and make some effort." But because she was a well-behaved and attractive child, her teachers and parents tended to overlook her learning needs. "She'll grow out of it," they said, not realizing that Joan needed much more specific help, not physical maturity. She was passed from grade to grade, but she knew she was falling farther behind her classmates each year. "Being passed along when you know you aren't learning does terrible things to your feelings about yourself," she says. "The only recognition I got was for my looks and personality, so by the time I reached high school, I had pretty much given up trying to get decent grades and I had started putting my time and energy into being Miss Popularity."

When Joan got to college, her excellent social skills were no substitute for understanding and completing assignments, for writing essays and term papers, for taking exams, or for participating in class discussions. It was only then that she realized how serious her learning difficulties had become. She flunked out of college, ashamed and depressed, believing that if only she had tried harder she would not have failed. Like many bright people who learn differently, she came to believe what she had been told so many times: She believed that her failure was entirely her own fault.

Fortunately for Joan, a family friend suggested that she take some educational and psychological tests.

The psychologist not only told me, but showed me, that I really am smart. She made me think about why I had had so many problems in school. At first, I kept repeating what everyone had been telling me, like "I'm just not motivated," and "Books just aren't my thing." But she made me see that just because I learn differently doesn't mean I can't learn. She helped me begin to understand that I can learn. Then, when I came to Landmark, I discovered that there are actual concrete steps that I can take to improve. I've learned how to organize, to take useful notes, to handle multiple-choice tests, to write a coherent essay. And the amazing thing is that the steps I have been taught are so obvious that I would think every student should be presented with them in high school.

Children whose language development is delayed also may grow up misunderstood, like Joan. If their invisible learning differences lead to problems in reading in the early elementary grades, the stage is set for unhappiness, frustration, and anger. The child who does not learn to decode words by the third grade almost invariably will encounter a broad range of learning problems.

The task of the child in the early grades is to learn to read. From about mid-third grade on through junior and senior high school, the task is to read in order to learn. If the student has not learned to read efficiently and with understanding, he will be unable to read for meaning in history, science, or literature. Typically, such students find themselves floundering in several subjects, since most junior and senior high school subjects depend on students' using textbooks as the main source of information on the subject. The chain reaction here follows this pattern:

- Early childhood—delayed language learning
- Primary grades—slow progress in learning to read and spell
- Upper elementary—poor grades in social studies, science, and other subjects that require considerable reading, spelling, and writing
- Junior high and beyond—diminished sense of worth, increased frustration, depression, or anger, all leading to more failure

But not all children who have learning differences fail to learn to read efficiently and accurately in the early grades. Some, like Eric, seem to catch on well and to read smoothly. He was talkative, curious, and successful in the primary grades, although he had some difficulty with spelling and writing. Eric did well in school until he had to do more writing, starting in the fifth grade.

> I was always trying to figure out how to say my thoughts and spell [them]. Somehow I couldn't get them from my brain to my fingers. I spent so much time trying to remember the order of the letters that I forgot what I was trying to say in my writing.

Eric, who had enjoyed reading and who usually could discuss what he had read, just couldn't take the next step. He could read and understand, but he stumbled when he had to retrieve and organize his thoughts and then write them out in correct spelling. When he was in primary classes, where he had lots of opportunities to share his thoughts and demonstrate his understanding by talking, Eric had the reputation of being a bright

child and a good student. But as the methods for prov-
ing his knowledge changed, and as he was required to
show what he knew less often by talking and more often
by writing, Eric's grades began to slip.

By the time Eric got to junior high school, he was
turned off by school. He hated teacher-centered learning, was bored in classes, and never handed in assignments. He loved music and the theater but avoided
academic coursework.

> I was so sick of hearing that I could do better if I'd just try
> that I was ready to drop out of school. I couldn't wait to
> be sixteen so I could quit. I read constantly but not
> schoolbooks. That's because I knew that anything I read
> in school I was going to have to write about. Every time I
> got a paper back, I could hardly see what I had written
> because of all my mistakes. I started making excuses for
> the work I wasn't doing, then basically stopped working.
> When I started to get into drugs, that's when I saw I had a
> problem.

The first red flags that Eric was setting up a chain
reaction were his difficulties with spelling and writing,
which did not interfere noticeably with his school performance until he reached the upper elementary grades.
By the time these things were recognized as important,
Eric had already developed a negative attitude toward
learning and had begun rejecting activities that he had
previously enjoyed. Eric's case suggests that parents
and teachers, without being alarmists, should pay attention to learning difficulties when they are first observed.
If these difficulties persist, they should be taken seri-

ously, and the student should have the type of assessment we discuss in the next chapter.

Children who learn differently may respond to their growing frustrations in school in a number of ways. Ted became an argumentative, insolent know-it-all. He grabbed every opportunity to put his teachers and parents down in unconscious retaliation for what he perceived to be *their* continual put-downs. Sue simply withdrew from participation to such an extent that teachers actually forgot she was in the classroom. This, of course, was just what she wanted. She sat quietly, caused no trouble, was always polite, never offered an answer or opinion, and never asked a question. She turned in assignments on time and handled them well enough to pass, but never well enough to approximate her very high academic potential. When hard-pressed, her teachers might recall her as "a nice quiet girl, not too bright, but doing her best." When shown her scores on an intelligence test, her English teacher said, "The test must be wrong. She is nowhere nearly that bright. Probably she's a good test taker."

Whether students hit learning barriers in third grade, high school, on the job, or in graduate school, those affected pay a high personal cost. Each community and the nation at large are losers when able students fail to learn. We lose the special contributions they could have made if they had been successful in school. We pay a high price when failure leads some of these bright young people to drugs, delinquency, or depression. For the individual, for Sue and Shawn, for Joan and Eric, and the millions they represent, that cost is paid many times over and in a variety of painful ways. Each will respond to the bumps in the learning road in ways that reflect their personalities, their life experiences, and the presence or absence of supportive or abusive adults in their lives. Most students who run into learning problems tell us stories like those we have reported.

Common threads in their experiences include the recognition that no matter how hard they try, they cannot meet the expectations set for them. They come to accept the judgments of the important people in their lives—parents, brothers and sisters, teachers—that they are (a) lazy or (b) stupid or (c) bad. They spend a lot of time trying to understand themselves and the world around them. They feel often that they will go through life disappointing themselves and others.

Over the years, the authors have known, worked with, and formed friendships with many adults who testify to the lifelong effects of these early feelings. Many of the adults—through their efforts and the support of caring parents, teachers, and mentors—have achieved success against long odds.

One such person, now a grandmother, still remembers with pain the day in fourth grade when her teacher told her parents that they should send her to a vocational school so she could become a domestic servant. She has advanced degrees in education and has had a distinguished career as a teacher and tutor of children and adults who learn differently. But she still has difficulty recognizing her worth. Another such person, a highly regarded sculptor, dropped out of a prestigious private school in his senior year. He could not continue to face the ridicule of students and teachers when his stammer blocked his ability to share his immense knowledge and humanistic insights in class. Fifty years later, encouraged to return to a reunion of his class, he wrote to a friend:

> I am really returning to make peace with myself.
> The anger in me has been that I was sent [to that
> school] to be and do something that I just couldn't
> do. I want to walk those old halls with the sense
> that I am—was—OK and that I, too, have suc-
> ceeded in my life "in my own way."

A creative and successful career woman and mother from a home with a caring family became so frustrated by her school environment that she spent her late teens and early twenties in exaggerated rebellion and recklessness. She combined substance abuse with demanding physical prowess in dangerous sports like hang gliding and white-water rafting. Today she is a top executive of a highly regarded learning-disabilities organization that she and two colleagues founded nearly fifteen years ago.

For each of these adults, ranging now in age from their mid-forties to mid-seventies, one of the biggest costs for having spent years in learning climates ill-suited to their needs has been the lifelong struggle to overcome the feeling that they are inferior. They find it difficult to accept the respect their families, clients, students, and communities give them readily. It is hard for them to see how much richness they have brought to those around them.

When children are misunderstood, when they do not receive the support they need to cope with the demands they face, and when they lose hope for their future, then what started out as learning differences are likely to develop into serious academic, social, behavioral, or self-image problems. Failure to recognize learning differences and take action constitutes the biggest problem of all. Yet when parents and teachers are sensi-

tive to these differences and address them early and
well, they can create a positive chain reaction by tap-
ping the creative talents and gifts of children who can
see and think about the world from a different perspective.

In a memoir, sculptor Malcolm Alexander con-
cluded:

> Many dyslexics have not been as fortunate as I.
> Many spend much of their lives in severe depres-
> sion, struggling endlessly, like Sisyphus, to roll
> their stone uphill. Too often they are rolling the
> wrong stone, as I did before fulfilling my dream.
> Some have succeeded in spite of their dyslexia.
> Each has a story not dissimilar to my own. And
> each of us has known that our difficulties were
> reduced to manageability only by the faith, the
> kindness, and the assistance of those exceptional
> "others" we have met along the way.

5. Taking the Mystery Out of Testing

> The only good thing about elementary school was testing. It was kind of a painful, drawn-out experience, but it really made me feel better about myself. They told me that I had high ability in a lot of areas, including general knowledge. It was the first time anyone ever told me I was smart.
>
> Brian Press

Academic and psychological testing has received mixed reviews in the popular and the educational press. Some negativism is justified by testing that is poorly conducted or test results that are improperly used, but well-trained, sensitive testers can be invaluable in determining an individual's potential for learning and in guiding his academic program and progress. Despite the problems, testing is the best system we have to assure that misunderstood and struggling learners get the help they need.

PROBLEMS WITH TESTING

"Shouldn't we have her tested?" is one of the first questions concerned parents and teachers ask when a student has trouble learning. Older students, those in high school and college, recount, with something bordering on either amazement or horror, the number of times they have been tested. They remember sitting with examiners, answering questions, drawing pictures, constructing designs with blocks, and fitting pegs into holes as part of the effort to find out what made them tick. Listening to student concerns provides insights that can guide parents, students, and examiners to avoid potential trouble spots and to make the most of the testing experience.

When students complain about their experiences, they often are quite specific about what they did not like:

- being tested in a hostile climate for the purpose of establishing who is to blame for their problems

- being left in the dark about why particular tests are being given, and what the test results and recommendations are

- being given a label as a result of the testing, with few if any recommendations about what steps to take to get effective help

- having testers focus almost exclusively on weaknesses, or present reports that consist of a litany of their weaknesses

- being tested at different times and under different conditions, producing conflicting results or diagnoses

- having reports filed in their permanent record that do not reflect an accurate understanding of their background, culture, and behavior and that lead later teachers to form preconceptions about their abilities

- perceiving that as a result of testing they have been robbed of what is positive in their lives—promotion to the next grade, participation in after-school activities or sports, or assignment to a regular class
- seeing little or no change in their performance or confidence as the result of the testing

MAKING ASSESSMENT WORK

Parents can help create a positive climate for assessment by explaining in language appropriate to the age and maturity of their children how it can help with these three critical needs:

- *Understanding*: Children need to understand themselves and how they learn in order to take control of the learning process. Parents and teachers who understand their children and their learning needs provide a secure environment and a strong foundation for growth.
- *Support*: Children need to know that they are not alone, that they have important adults who care about them. They and their parents need to know what kind of help they need and where to go to get it.
- *Hope*: No matter how poor their performance has been, children need to believe in themselves and to look for a brighter future. They need parents and teachers to see them not as students who will "never amount to anything" but as young people capable of change and growth.

"Assessment" or "diagnostic assessment" may be better terms to describe this experience than "testing." To many students, testing implies right and wrong answers, success and failure, victory and defeat. Without as many negative connotations, "assessment" is a good word for the whole evaluation process, one part of which is testing. The purpose of assessment is not simply to diagnose problems, but to gain a deeper understanding of how a person learns. Ideally, assessment should give as much attention to examining students' strengths as to identifying their weaknesses. Most students with learning problems respond well when their strengths and interests are explored, especially as resources for addressing their weaker areas.

Testing must, of course, directly and honestly explore students' weaknesses in order to uncover the underlying reasons for their difficulties. While knowing the cause does not solve the problem, it provides important clues for planning students' academic programs and encouraging their social growth. In addition to diagnosing a problem, if it exists, an assessment should provide a clear description of the difficulty and how it affects performance, and a prescription, or course of action, for addressing it.

An assessment report isn't an educational plan, but it should provide enough information to allow teachers and parents to make informed choices about methods of teaching and management of difficulties at home. Additionally, a good assessment can establish a base line for judging student progress. The report will record the current levels of various academic skills and will usually recommend a time line for retesting specific areas. Thus it serves as an important tool for monitoring and measuring students' growth and determining the effectiveness of particular teaching methods or programs.

To interpret test results accurately, the examiner must collect and review as much information as possible about the particular student and his behavior in both school and nonschool settings. Parents, teachers, employers, coaches, club leaders, and the student himself can provide valuable insights that can make the interpretation of results more useful. When such information is gathered with care, the examiner is likely to understand the student more completely and to recognize that the student's behavior in the testing situation represents only one facet of his personality.

The student should be an active participant in all phases of the assessment process, including the conference that reports the results and recommendations, in a way that is appropriate for his age and maturity. When the student is at the center of the educational partnership that includes his parents and teachers, he is better able to accept and understand his strengths and weaknesses, his rights and responsibilities, and to respond to good teaching by working hard. Being a central partner provides the student with the information and experience he needs to become a responsible advocate for himself.

In summary, assessment is critically important if it is used to help us think diagnostically about the problems a student has. Tests are of little value and may even be harmful when they are used only to label and sort students. Assessment results should be considered as one piece of a puzzle, not "the answer" to "the problem." In planning instructional programs, teachers, counselors, school psychologists, parents, and students should look at all the evidence they have.

ASSESSMENT

Gathering Background Information

Effective assessment, whether by an individual examiner or a team of specialists, begins with gathering information from people who know the student best, both in areas where he succeeds and in areas where he does not. This information is typically obtained through observations, questionnaires, inventories, and interviews and from sources such as existing records and reports. Parents and teachers need to ensure that the child's interests, strengths, and talents, as well as his weaknesses, are clearly represented in these records. The student himself is often a source of valuable information. This is particularly true of older students, but even young children may be able to tell how and why they perform the way they do.

Parents are often asked to provide or to obtain information about the child's growth and development, with particular attention to his birth, the events of his infancy and early childhood, his medical history, his social and emotional development, and his school history. Frank reporting by parents is critical if there is to be a thorough assessment of the learner. Accurate medical, developmental, and social/emotional histories are key in ruling out or pinpointing other factors that affect learning in important ways.

In addition to providing this personal information, parents can make the assessment process more meaningful by giving examiners a written statement that details why they want their child to be tested. This statement should contain a list of questions and concerns, specific problems they would like addressed, and a general description of what they hope to learn from the experience.

Types of Testing

There are several major categories of tests that form the basis of a typical diagnosis. There are tests of achievement, which examine the student's knowledge of academic information in the various subject areas, such as reading, composition, arithmetic, and spelling. There are also psychological tests, which include tests of aptitude (usually referred to as IQ tests) and tests of emotional and social adjustment. The latter are generally used when a student's withdrawn or disruptive behavior suggests that learning may be affected by nonacademic issues.

A common reason for testing a student is to find out whether he is eligible for help or for special accommodations in school, such as having extra time or special assistance in class or on tests. Although specific guidelines vary, the typical methods of determining the student's eligibility involve testing to see if there is a discrepancy between aptitude and achievement or between grade level and achievement. If a student's achievement in one or more subjects falls considerably below what is expected of students in his grade or with his aptitude, he is likely to be a good candidate for receiving special help or program modifications. The diagnostician selects, scores, and compares tests to make this determination.

But the kind of assessment that is most useful in planning a student's program seeks to find out much more than the discrepancy between achievement and aptitude or grade level. This testing evaluates the functions (such as language, memory, and attention) discussed in the earlier chapters of this book to discover whether problems in these areas are contributing to difficulties in school. It explores questions such as: Does this student have trouble with short-term, long-term, or active working memory? How effectively is he paying attention? Does this student have difficulty following verbal directions? How does he learn best? What is interfering with his learning? What abilities does he have that he can use to compensate for his problems?

To use tests effectively and gain a detailed understanding of the student, diagnosticians look beyond the quantitative results (test scores) to the qualitative information they can obtain. A skilled examiner is as interested in observing how the student approaches each task as he is with the results of the tests.

When the test has been administered and scored according to established procedures, he may follow up with comments and questions ("That was great! How did you solve it?") or with variations in test administration ("I'd like to try that one again, but this time I want you to repeat the question out loud before you try to answer it"). In this way, examiners not only gain valuable information, they also communicate to the student their genuine interest in him and how he learns.

WHAT IS INTELLIGENCE?

In recent years a number of thoughtful educators and researchers have raised important questions about relying on aptitude (IQ) tests in isolation when determining students' ability to learn.

Howard Gardner, an eminent Harvard University psychologist, is the best known of these critics of our limited view of intelligence. We all know people who can tear an engine apart, tinker with it, and put it back together so that it runs like new. We have colleagues who can walk into a room of strangers and instinctively sense the atmosphere and respond to it. Some people think three-dimensionally and can visualize what landscapes and buildings will look like just by studying maps and blueprints. These kinds of intelligences are seldom acknowledged in our language-dependent schools, but they are critical in making society work.

According to Gardner, there are at least seven distinct kinds of intelligence that we have in varying degrees. Only two of these—verbal, or linguistic, and mathematical-logical intelligence—are reflected to any significant extent in current school programs.

In his book, *Frames of Mind,* Gardner proposes that in addition to linguistic and mathematical-logical intelligences, there are five equally valuable kinds of intelligence. These are *musical intelligence*, which many talented people have and which Mozart had in spades; *spatial intelligence*, which leads people into careers as painters, sculptors, surgeons, engineers, architects, mechanics, or navigators; *bodily kinesthetic intelligence*, the ability to use your hands, mouth, foot, or entire body to do things both practical and creative, an ability shared by dancers, athletes, and craftspeople; *interpersonal intelligence*, the intelligence that helps us understand other people and plays a major role in the success of teachers, salesmen, politicians, counselors, and the clergy; and finally, *intrapersonal intelligence*, the degree to which we gain understanding of ourselves and use it constructively to deal with our lives.

Gardner emphasizes that all of these intelligences exist, in varying degrees, within most of us. He also says that "being strong in one intelligence has no particular implication about strength in other intelligences."

Gardner and others have helped educators to think more globally about the nature of intelligence. In the future, we may have tests and teaching methods that better assess and capitalize on the diverse expressions of intelligence. For now, the most commonly used aptitude tests continue to focus on linguistic and mathematical abilities. There is growing emphasis by examiners, however, on exploring the ways students approach tasks and solve problems, and on looking at qualitative as well as quantitative factors in student performance—in other words, at *how* they perform a task, not just what their score is.

Evaluation by a Multidisciplinary Team

In most instances, students are first tested by a single specialist, either in school or in a clinic or private educational or psychological practice. For many students, the information obtained this way is sufficient for modifying the academic program to meet their needs. In some cases, however, the nature of the problem calls for testing by a multidisciplinary team.

A multidisciplinary team includes specialists who bring their varied knowledge and experience—their "multiple intelligences"—to the evaluation process.

They look for interconnections and interrelationships to help formulate recommendations. Their perspectives make possible a broad understanding of the nature and underlying causes of the student's difficulties.

ROLES OF MULTIDISCIPLINARY TEAM MEMBERS

The specialists students may expect to meet in the course of a multidisciplinary assessment include psychologists, speech and language pathologists, neuropsychologists, and/or educational specialists. Sometimes the team will consult with neurologists, audiologists, ophthalmologists, and social workers. Typically the assessment team members each carry out specific types of testing.

- The psychologist is responsible for evaluating intellectual ability and emotional adjustment. For intellectual ability, she generally uses an intelligence test that is administered individually, such as the Wechsler Intelligence Scale, the Stanford-Binet, or the Woodcock Johnson Psycho-Educational Battery. These tests provide subscores for a variety of functions (e.g., word knowledge, short-term memory) that the test identifies as components of intellectual ability.

  To evaluate a student's emotional adjustment, the psychologist may use several methods, such as interviews, questionnaires, inventories, and projective tests (for example, telling stories or describing pictures or designs). Students who experience academic problems are at risk for developing social, emotional, or behavioral problems, as discussed in Chapter 4. School takes up much of their lives, and in school they are expected to learn and are judged on how well they do so. The child's success or lack of success in this first important job outside the home profoundly affects his sense of self, and this, in turn, can affect his later performance in school.

- A speech-and-language pathologist often is an important member of the team—he deals with many aspects of learning that are central to school success. He understands and looks for the relationship between language and intelligence and that between language and learning. He is especially useful in evaluating students who struggle with reading or listening comprehension, or who have trouble conveying ideas in speech or writing. The speech and language tests he uses assess language functions that are either not covered or are covered in less depth by intelligence tests. Because language ability is basic to learning and to all communication, the issues that the speech/language pathologist discovers in his assessment are especially important.

- A neuropsychologist looks at learning as a function of the brain. The tests she uses explore such brain functions as memory, attention, sequential processing, and motor abilities that are not fully assessed by intelligence tests. The neuropsychologist gleans from her tests descriptive information about the way the student learns. She is sensitive to the ways in which functions of the brain interrelate, and thus she may be able to offer many helpful suggestions about ways the student can use his strengths to compensate for his weaknesses.

- A special educator (given several different titles, such as educational specialist, resource-room specialist, generic special educator) looks at the student's achievement in relation to the range of academic skills he needs for his age and grade. These skills include decoding and reading comprehension, spelling, handwriting, composition, arithmetical computation and problem-solving skills, study skills, time management, and recognizing and using appropriate strategies.

  Achievement in specific academic skills— such as reading, spelling, and math—are usually reported as grade levels or percentile scores. A grade-level score indicates that the student in that subject has performed on the test at the same level as the average student of that grade; percentile score indicates the percent of students at his grade he has surpassed on that test. A percentile score of 73 in arithmetic computation received by a fourth-grader tells us that he answered correctly more questions than 73 percent of the large number of fourth-graders who were used to establish the standards for the test.

  Because it is harder to measure more complex skills, such as time management and organization, the special educator may turn to more qualitative means—such as surveys and interviews, portfolios of student work, teacher observations, and informal tests and exercises—to assess them.

- Other specialists are generally called on when there are specific problems that fall in the realm of their specialties. A neurologist looks at such problems as seizures or sleep disorders. A psychiatrist reviews cases where depression, anorexia, or other serious emotional symptoms are seen. Vision and hearing losses may be reviewed by the ophthalmologist and audiologist, while family conflicts may be helped by a social worker trained in family issues.

A complete evaluation by a multidisciplinary team usually takes a full day or more. When the testing is completed, the team generally meets to discuss their findings, decide whether a specific diagnosis can be made, develop a comprehensive description of the student as a learner, make recommendations, and establish a follow-up plan. This discussion forms the basis for a written report and a conference with the student and parent.

REPORTING AND USING EVALUATION RESULTS

Assessment Conference

When the assessment is complete, the examiner or the team members whose specialties are most relevant to the student generally schedule a meeting with the parents and/or the student. Depending on the age and maturity of the student, his role in the conference will vary. Often this meeting takes place before the written report is completed, so the results and recommendations are made orally. Parents and the student need ample time to ask questions and to engage in discussion about the findings.

Although the written report is the most lasting product of an educational assessment, what students remember most is the time spent with the examiner during the testing and at the conference that follows.

Spending a day with a caring and well-trained diagnostician who gives each student his full attention can
be an enlightening experience. The culminating conference, in which the examiner explains and interprets the
test results objectively, can give the student an entirely
new perspective on himself. Fine diagnosticians set the
stage for a student to take a fresh look at himself in these
ways:

- carefully observing the student's efforts, listening to his ideas and insights, and incorporating
  them into the content of the conference;
- treating the student with respect and acknowl-
  edging that he plays the central role in his educational future;
- explaining the student's strengths and weaknesses honestly, using examples, analogies, and
  simple, clear language;
- circumscribing and limiting the student's problems so the student sees them as manageable
  rather than as overwhelming;
- describing ways the student can use his
  strengths to improve weak areas and ways he can
  develop his strengths further (older students, for
  example, often find it useful to learn about successful adults who think and approach problems
  in the same way they do);
- recommending kinds of support and accommodations he is eligible for and explaining how
  to receive them; describing the student's responsibilities in dealing with his problems; and discussing what he can do and to whom he can turn
  when he is confused or discouraged;
- suggesting follow-up procedures—such as re-

testing and reviewing student work—to see what is working and what is not, and building the student's efforts and observations into that process.

The posttesting conference is one of the best ways for a student to become self-aware and to gain understanding and hope. The very fact of the assessment demonstrates that there are caring people who will support him in his efforts to improve.

What a Good Assessment Report Contains

Whether the student is tested by a single specialist or by a multidisciplinary team, the results should be summarized in writing in clear, jargon-free language. Those who are not specialists (older students, parents, and regular education teachers) should be able to understand the findings and recommendations. They are the ones most affected by the results. When technical terms must be used, the report should define them clearly, using practical examples whenever possible.

The report should be comprehensive, honest, and optimistic in tone. It should summarize the reasons for referral, background information, test results (including scores and observations), diagnosis (if appropriate), description of the student, recommendations, and plans for follow-up.

If testing reveals a problem, a good report identifies it, giving it a name (diagnosis) if appropriate, a definition, and description ("By dyslexia, we mean . . ."). The report also circumscribes the diagnosis by explaining what the problem is not ("Dyslexia is not caused by lack of intelligence").

The report should include a thorough description of the student's specific learning strengths and weaknesses and explain any patterns or connection among them. For example, if the student's weakness appears to be "poor motivation," the report might explain this by identifying the underlying causes of this behavior, such as inadequate skills and chronic failure.

Having isolated the apparent causes of the problems, a useful report then goes on to make programmatic recommendations by listing and describing suitable teaching methods, curriculum materials, and learning methods that have a history of success with similar students. The report includes recommendations for all interested parties—teachers, parents, and student—along with guidelines for measuring progress and suggestions for regular follow-up.

Using the Information

When a problem is identified, the most immediate and common benefit for students, parents, and teachers is a tremendous sense of relief. A diagnosis helps to define and limit the problem, and it builds the foundation for hope by laying to rest many of the fears the student has harbored. Most students, even those who have not been called names, have developed an explanation for their difficulties—"I'm dumb" being the most common and damaging one. Parents and teachers worry about the dangers of diagnostic "labels," but they should balance these realistic concerns against the potential positive results for the child. A diagnosis is often more helpful, more empowering, and more limited in scope than the informal, often demeaning labels like "lazy" or "stupid" that will substitute for it in the absence of an assessment.

The diagnosis can become the first step in finding understanding and help. There are increasing sources of specific help for children and adults who have a specific, identified problem (dyslexia, learning disability, attention deficit–hyperactivity disorder). Many of these resources are detailed in the Appendixes of this book.

There are a number of practical and legal benefits of diagnosis. The student may be eligible for special instructional programs, either in the regular classroom or in a specialized setting. Programs available in most schools include tutorial or small-group instruction, academic and behavioral counseling, and in-class accommodations and program modifications. To be eligible for such services, a student must be diagnosed according to certain criteria, specified by state and federal laws and regulations.

Since these criteria vary somewhat from state to state, it is important to discover how eligibility is determined where the child attends school. Prior to an assessment conference, parents should find out as much as possible about what criteria are applied so they can ensure that the assessment report provides the information necessary for determining eligibility.

There are also risks that accompany naming the problem. Some students, though relieved to know the nature of the problem and what they can do about it, are justifiably reluctant to participate in support services and programs, particularly those that take them away from classmates or activities they enjoy. They may resist participating in programs that they fear will lead to teasing or name calling. Many students and their parents worry that teachers, administrators, and employers will use the diagnosis to limit expectations for educational, personal, and professional growth. Advocacy by parents, a topic that is beyond the scope of this book, includes an exploration of community resources and of the laws that guarantee an appropriate education and safeguard against discrimination in school and on the job.

These include the Individuals with Disabilities Education Act, known as IDEA; the Rehabilitation Act of 1973, section 504, often referred to simply as section 504; and the Americans with Disabilities Act, or the ADA. Many of the organizations listed in the Appendixes of this book provide excellent information regarding advocacy issues.

An assessment may occasionally result in an accurate diagnosis that parents, teachers, or the student are reluctant to accept. Alternatively, testing results may contradict the perceptions of a parent or teacher who knows the child intimately. In these cases, seeking a second opinion is advisable. Parents may wish to explore their right to obtain such an assessment under the provisions of the IDEA.

The positive effects that good testing can have in setting the student on the road to self-understanding and academic growth far outweigh the negative results that may be associated with it. As long as students learn what their strengths and weaknesses are, how they can address their weak areas, how they can get the help they need, and how they can look to the future with hope, they can reap enormous benefits from the assessment experience.

6. What Works in School

From the day children enter preschool or kindergarten, at age three to five, until they leave school, whether at the earliest age possible or after completing graduate school, their lives and their feelings about themselves are, to a large extent, influenced by the demands of school and the expectations of their teachers. Parents who discover and understand, in more than a general way, how teaching and learning can work together are in a good position to give their children informed support as they face the challenges that school presents.

To provide that support and to serve as effective advocates, parents need to know how schools and teachers can address the needs of students who learn differently. They need to know what works and what does not work for their children. They need this knowledge so they can be informed participants in choosing the next year's teacher; in guiding the selection of courses and schedules; in evaluating the effectiveness of tutoring, special courses, teaching techniques, or programs; and in supporting their children and the teachers who work with them.

In this chapter, we use Landmark College as a model of teaching that addresses the needs of students who learn differently. The principles and practices we will discuss have proved to be effective for many students with academic difficulties. There is nothing magic about them. Teachers at any level can adapt and apply these principles. In fact, most of what follows describes efficient, organized, thoughtful instruction that puts into practice long-accepted teaching principles. Most students, not only those who learn differently, benefit when instruction is based on the ideas and approaches we set forth here.

Additionally, by looking at ways teachers put sound educational principles into practice, parents can gain insights into ways they can adapt life in the home to the learning needs of their children. Let's look at the principles of effective teaching on which Landmark College bases its instruction, review some of the teaching techniques employed, and examine the Master Notebook study system Landmark uses with all students.

Effective Teaching: Principles and Practices

GAPS, HOLES, AND ASSUMPTIONS

Students develop academic skills at different rates, depending on the subject, their abilities, their interest in it, and the quality of instruction. They may perform very well in some areas and on some tasks and do poorly in others. Students whose mastery of skills is characterized by unevenness and who have gaps in ba-

sic skills are likely to find schoolwork hard or to progress more slowly than would be expected from their
level of intelligence. A student who, for example, is a
poor reader but has strong listening skills may be able to
keep up in elementary and secondary school. By attending carefully to lectures and class discussions, he learns
what is required. When he gets to college, however, he
may fail in courses that require extensive independent
reading. This student could choose to use "bypass"
techniques, such as books on tape. But to succeed in
these courses, as well as in the working world, where
tapes are often unavailable for day-to-day use, he must
find out what skills he lacks and seek systematic instruction to fill in the holes.

When students struggle in school, neither parents,
teachers, nor the students themselves should make un-
supported assumptions about the students' skills. Not
infrequently, the poor reader who listens well is able to
mask from himself, his parents, and his teachers the fact
that he lacks basic reading skills. When parents and
teachers focus their concern on understanding where
the child is rather than on where they think he should
be, they can avoid the painful misunderstandings im-
plicit in such statements as "You're not trying hard
enough," "You knew it yesterday," and "If only you'd
apply yourself." Instead, they can help students to address their problems by finding Point Zero.

POINT ZERO

If we think of the sequence of skills on which an athlete
depends, we can usually identify the spots where those
skills break down. A baseball player, for example, who

is in a batting slump, has to discover where the "weak link" is in the chain of motions that make up his batting. It may be that his grip on the bat is inefficient, so he is swinging too early or too late, too high or too low. He may need to relearn the correct grip in order to improve his total performance. In his case, his grip on the bat is point zero. No matter how accomplished he may be, an athlete often has to go back to fundamentals in order to keep his performance at the highest level possible.

For students, locating and starting at the point where they are, both in knowledge of content and in skill, is the first step. James Baucom, Landmark's Academic Dean, calls this "beginning at point zero." With younger students, teachers can often locate the necessary starting point quickly. This can be done by combining observations with inventory testing and reviewing student work. The place to begin instruction is at the weakest point in the chain of skills required for successful performance.

These same means of finding the place to start may be used with older students, but finding it may require more time, since students must use complicated chains of skills for most secondary school tasks. As students go through school, they acquire bits and pieces of information, some organized but many that are poorly integrated with other knowledge. As a result, it may be difficult to determine what level they are on and why their performance is breaking down. On the other hand, older students often can provide more information about what they know and where they are having trouble.

By targeting the problem while respecting the student's ability to perform and to grow in the areas of his strengths, teachers and parents encourage independence. When the student receives direct instruction that uses his strong learning channels to shore up areas of weakness, he usually makes more rapid progress. Students of all ages need good teaching at the point (point zero) where their understanding falters, and systematic practice at the point (point zero) where their skills are not yet automatic. At the same time, parents and teachers need to guard against underestimating students' skills in other areas.

EXPECTATIONS, SUPPORT, AND ACCOUNTABILITY

> When I was in high school, every time I was assigned a paper to write, I panicked. I'd run home to my mother crying, "I can't do it, I can't do it." So she tried to help me, but actually she ended up practically writing the paper. I still have trouble, but now when I get a writing assignment, I go to my tutor and she gives me the push I need to get started. For example, we may work on an outline together. Then I can go on my own and complete the assignment independently.
>
> Stephanie

Stephanie and her tutor know that she is not yet ready to be entirely independent, but they also know that she can be much more independent than she has been in the past. Her tutor works with her, not for her, in preparing the outline and then expects her to take that outline and develop it on her own.

Among the hardest decisions parents and teachers confront as they work with students whose work is uneven are setting reasonable expectations, providing the right amount of support, and holding students accountable for all they can do. While students need direct instruction and lots of practice at point zero, they also need to rely on their better-developed skills to do as much work as possible independently.

In the effort to be supportive, adults may fall into the trap of overestimating weaknesses or underestimating strengths. When we overestimate a student's weaknesses, he may feel he is being placed at point zero in all areas when, in fact, he needs that support in only one or two areas. He may become angry or resistant, believing, "They all think I'm dumb." Similarly, the student who finds an academic task too difficult because he lacks necessary skills and background knowledge finds little satisfaction when the help he gets allows him only to complete the immediate task at hand and fails to fill in those gaps that are creating the problems he is having.

Parents and teachers may feel as if they are walking on a tightrope, trying to balance between asking students to do what they cannot yet do and doing for them what they are capable of doing on their own. Good diagnostic testing and the observations of good teachers are the best means for locating the boundaries between what the student should be expected to do and where he needs continued support.

MULTISENSORY TEACHING AND LEARNING

In the case of learning sound-symbol relationships, a basic reading skill, we advised having students say the letter and its sound as they write it, thus engaging hearing, doing, seeing, and feeling to reinforce one another.

This approach (simplified in this summary) is called multisensory. When various senses are called into play, many students are better able to understand and remember the material.

Put yourself in the student's place by thinking about some information new to you that was presented in such a way that you can recall it easily. Perhaps it was a lecture or workshop you attended where the presenter not only talked but also used good visual material to illustrate his key points, and perhaps also had you act out a role that demonstrated your grasp of those points. Perhaps it was a nature walk with a park ranger who took you beyond what he could present in a lecture hall and gave you direct experience with the things he talked about.

Multisensory instruction that combines teacher talk and student reading with other activities and materials is more often found in elementary schools and graduate schools than in the years between. At the elementary level, students are likely to engage in discussion, work on projects, and go on field trips; graduate programs often use laboratory work, seminars, and work experiences to establish learning firmly. At the middle school, high school, and undergraduate college levels, students are less likely to have these multisensory learning experiences.

Effective multisensory instruction is focused and well organized. No student, least of all those with learning difficulties, gets much of value from a wandering discussion, a field trip without a clear purpose, or a cluttered, confusing chart or diagram. Unless multisensory experiences reinforce the key concepts the student is expected to learn, they have little merit. In multisensory instruction, the presentation of material provides that reinforcement and support, without confusing or "upstaging" the information.

Computer software programs, interactive videos, and other multimedia products hold considerable promise. They can enhance instruction and clarify content in new and challenging ways. It is important, however, not to assume that all multimedia presentations provide effective multisensory instruction. Effective instruction is interactive and capitalizes on the sensitivity of the various learning channels without bombarding or overloading them. It involves the student as an active participant, rather than a passive receiver of information.

UNDERSTANDING, LEARNING, AND REMEMBERING

We have said a lot about the importance of establishing skills as a foundation for success in school. Important as these skills are, particularly the language skills and the study skills, in order for them to become useful tools for students, the students must see that the skills have meaning beyond themselves. For this reason, at each step students should be guided to see that there is a logical structure in what they are studying and that understanding that structure helps in retaining the information.

The student who learns the rules, patterns, and structures that prevail in the various subjects has a distinct advantage when he faces new material, particularly if he has a weakness in another area. For instance, the student whose visual memory is weak often has trouble remembering how to spell words, but if spelling words are presented in groups that share certain structural characteristics *(enough, rough, tough),* or that follow certain rules (how to add suffixes to root words), he may find them easier to remember.

When students learn the logical organization—the rules, patterns, and concepts—on which a particular area of study is based, they find it easier to pay attention, to remember, and to automatize. Further, they are learning more than just the specific information presented. As they see analogies with other areas of learning, they can apply what they know to these new fields.

Many teachers do an excellent job of explaining the structure of the explicit curriculum, giving students a clear picture of how it is organized. A history teacher, for example, may point out the several ways in which historians select and present information—for instance, by topic, by chronology, or by cause-and-effect relationships.

There is also an invisible curriculum that underlies all learning, and students who learn differently may need special help in learning this curriculum. It consists, in part, of the structure of oral and written language, the patterns and concepts on which study skills depend, and ways to organize information and improve memory. Students learn best when teachers address this "invisible curriculum" by teaching the skills that support learning.

A NEW TAKE ON MISTAKES

Regarding mistakes positively is one of the most important gifts parents and teachers can give to children. Their mistakes are good clues to how they are learning, where their understanding breaks down, and what they need to do to get beyond the mistake. Perhaps they need to break the information into smaller units. Perhaps they made unrealistic assumptions about the extent of their understanding. Whatever the reason, parents and teachers should view students' mistakes as important feedback and should encourage students to analyze and learn from them.

The accuracy of guided missiles and other automatic piloting devices relies on built-in error-detection devices. These analyze the errors occurring during flight and use them to guide the flight course. Errors here are recognized as an integral part of the process and as checkpoints leading to accuracy. In the same way, teacher, parents, and students themselves can use mistakes as mechanisms for correcting the course so that students can reach their learning goals on time and on target.

THE GIFT OF TIME

Pacing instruction to match the student's rate of learning by covering material neither too rapidly nor too slowly is a hallmark of fine teaching.

If we compare education to making a journey, we see that what we learn along the way is as important as reaching our destination or goal (graduating or getting a good grade). If we live in Boston and are making a journey to Seattle, how we get there and how long it takes will vary depending on what we want to accomplish along the way, as well as our choice of transportation, our resources, and external factors, such as weather and road conditions. If we encounter problems, such as bad weather or mechanical breakdowns, along the way, or if we get lost, we must be willing to make adjustments—perhaps traveling a little longer each day or adjusting our time of arrival.

The student who described his learning disability as "a monster that eats time" put his finger on one of the greatest burdens carried by many students who learn differently. Some specific ways parents and teachers can ease this burden include:

- presenting material without rushing, using natural pauses and allowing time for questions
- providing extra time for students to speak and to formulate answers to questions
- allowing extra time for completing quizzes and exams
- giving shorter, more frequent assignments
- spacing due dates for assignments throughout the term, rather than having them all due at the end
- extending the time required to complete a course, program, or degree

When parents and teachers give a gift of time, they affirm for students the value of spending more time. Students who are given an opportunity to complete tasks at a pace they can handle and who form a habit of putting in extra time will develop the discipline of hard work—a crucial factor in success for all students with learning difficulties.

THE MICRO-UNIT

Many students are confused and overwhelmed when large amounts of information are presented to them at once. But when complicated concepts or processes are presented in a sequence of smaller, interrelated chunks, students generally can grasp the meaning of the whole.

Breaking complex ideas and processes into their component parts is called "micro-uniting." This approach is widely used in business, industry, and daily life. Step-by-step directions for programming and readying a computer for operation is an example of micro-uniting, as is the detailed checklist that airline pilots must follow when preparing to take off or land. Micro-uniting, breaking material into manageable parts, is a powerful tool for tackling difficult assignments.

In the academic setting, teachers who are successful in teaching challenging material often apply the micro-uniting process. For example, rather than assigning a research paper due at a distant date, they may require students to complete one section at a time, perhaps submitting the topic and list of resources first, then a tentative outline, note cards for each major heading in the outline next, and so on. For this to be useful to students, teachers need to give feedback at each step along the way. This prevents students from feeling overwhelmed, gives students and teachers opportunities to evaluate progress, section by section, and promotes good time management.

Students learn to work in micro-units when teachers model this process in their instruction. For example, the basic building block for writing an essay is the paragraph. For students who do not understand how to construct a paragraph, having the elements that make up a paragraph isolated and taught in sequence may be necessary.

Micro-Uniting and Critical Thinking

Micro-uniting encourages students and teachers to think critically about the processes and practices they use in teaching and learning. Teachers frequently ask themselves, "Why am I teaching this concept or process in this order? Does this subpoint I am making support the skill, topic, or concept I am teaching? How can I break this complicated issue into parts that students can understand readily?" For their part, students, given information in manageable chunks, progress from superficial analysis to deeper understanding. Using a series of clear steps, they discover that they can complete tasks that previously defeated them. Once a student learns how to break down an advanced assignment, such as writing a three-page essay on a controversial topic, he may surprise himself and his teachers by the quality of his response.

Micro-Uniting and Time Management

The micro-unit is also a strong weapon for fighting procrastination. Facing a major task often is overwhelming. We cannot see how we will ever complete it. So, in many cases, we put off tackling it all. Then, as the deadline approaches, we scurry around, work around the clock, and produce something just to meet the deadline. Even those people who claim to work best under the pressure of time pay a price for the stress they inflict on themselves by waiting until the last minute.

Students have to plan their time when they have a distant due date for a major paper or examination. They can do this by breaking the assignment into micro-units and listing all the tasks they must do to complete the assignment. Then they review the list and decide in which order they should do the tasks. The first task in preparing a term paper may be doing research in the library and the last task typing or printing the final draft. In between are such tasks as taking notes, preparing an outline, writing a first draft, revising, and rewriting.

To gain control over this assignment, the student works backward from the due date. If the paper is due on March 30, he is encouraged to schedule producing the final draft on March 28. Then he estimates the time he will need for revising and sets the date for starting that piece of work. Because his other appointments and commitments are also recorded on his calendar, he can be more realistic about the time he can devote to each of the tasks. It takes time and practice, as well as coaching by teachers, for students to master this system of time management, but with each attempt they gain in their ability to cope with typical college-level assignments. How much more efficient it would be if they learned these skills in high school or earlier!

STUDENTS' INTERESTS AND EXPERTISE

Capitalizing on students' interests and areas of expertise to support academic learning is a particularly effective teaching technique. The student who does not grasp the concept of the micro-unit when his teacher presents it may be unaware that he is already applying that concept in his nonacademic activities. If he is an accomplished basketball player, for example, he knows he must practice regularly, whether he feels like it or not. Because he wants to improve, he listens carefully to the coach as he demonstrates the skills each play requires. If he is having trouble with his jump shot, he learns to analyze all of its components: the placement of his feet, his grip on the ball, the orientation of his shoulders, the direction of the jump, and the release and follow-through. By breaking the play down, he discovers where he needs to put his efforts if he hopes to improve and to perform at his best.

A student with a strong interest and ability in athletics, art, drama, or any other field is likely to be more receptive to seeing that academic learning is analogous to these interests in its requirements. Analogy is a potent learning tool and can be used with more abstract concepts as well. Comparing transitional words in writing to the rocks in a river draws a clear picture for the student who likes canoeing or kayaking. The kayaker has to pay close attention to the rocks in order to "read" the water's flow and to navigate safely and smoothly. The reader, in the same way, needs to watch for linguistic signals indicating when and how the flow of the writer's ideas has changed direction.

AUTOMATIZATION

If students learn to use mistakes constructively; to break learning into small steps; to see the rules and patterns in what they are learning; and to do for themselves all that they can do; they are well on the way to gaining a solid understanding of the material they are studying. When they understand language skills, study skills, and basic facts and information, and file them properly in long-term memory, students have the foundation for developing more advanced learning skills. But advanced skills—like note taking, writing, and reading—require students to think critically, analyze, summarize, and draw conclusions at the same time that they decode, write, spell, or type. Only when the basic skills are automatic can students give their attention and energy to higher-level thinking skills. We say that a skill is automatized when we can call on it and use it while the focus of our attention is directed elsewhere.

Automatization is an important concept for teachers, parents, and students to understand. To promote mastery, teachers (and parents can support this) can build in time regularly for the student to practice using information or skills beyond the point that he understands them. Athletes accept the well-established necessity of practicing something that they already understand. In school, such practice is often shrugged off as meaningless drill. Yet without the mastery that comes with practice, those who learn differently will not become the students they are capable of being. Thoughtful practice, rather than mindless drill, is the key.

If a student's reading skills, for example, lag behind his ability to comprehend ideas or his writing skills are inadequate for conveying his thoughts, he will become increasingly hampered in school and college. This weak link in his skills necessarily detracts from his ability to use higher-level skills and to achieve at the level of his understanding, so the student needs to concentrate on making these fundamental skills as automatic as possible.

To reach this goal, the student must allocate sufficient time to practice certain fundamental skills until he has "overlearned" them. Sometimes, even when he has mastered them, he may need to review and practice them. While skills learned are seldom lost, when they are used infrequently they may need a period of more intense practice to bring them back to the level of the automatic. Ask any baseball player heading back to spring training.

THE LEARNING SPIRAL

The micro-unit is the seed from which learning grows. As one step is mastered, students build on it to master the next, in an ever-growing and more complex spiral. Students learn what is meant by topic sentence, supporting details, and summary sentence, and the various uses of the paragraph, through direct instruction and practice. Over time, they come to understand these elements and forms and can write an effective paragraph. Later, they move logically to the next bend in the spiral. This may be the essay containing several paragraphs. Then, they learn about introductory paragraphs, transitions from paragraph to paragraph, different ways to express the main idea, and forceful conclusions.

As students master skills and learn concepts, they discover a strong link between what they learned yesterday and what they are introduced to today. This return, review, and extension we can think of as forming a spiral of learning.

Spiraling capitalizes on what the student has already learned by relating it to what he is now trying to learn. It includes review and repetition of prior material, but it involves much more than that. It takes discrete information or specific skills and puts them to use in varying contexts, each of which has its own purpose.

Thus spiraling is a means of applying skills and information in ways that reinforce and diversify them. On their own, some students are unlikely to see the variety of possible applications for information and skills. They can learn to do so through "spiraling" instruction that provides such guidance over an extended period of time.

TANGIBLE SUCCESSES

Self-esteem is built on genuine, tangible successes. As long as expectations reflect realistically what the student can accomplish, the student should be held accountable for achieving them. If he fails to do so, we must reevaluate to determine where the failure lies. When he is successful, the student begins to see hope for future successes, using each positive experience to build toward the next. This process is a continuous one.

Each of the principles discussed above contributes to the student's progress toward his goals. At each step along the way—as he gains understanding of the structure of the material to be learned, breaks difficult content and concepts into micro-units, and practices skills to the point of automatization—the student will enjoy honest success and satisfaction. If he likens this process to climbing a mountain, the student can see that going step by step, building each step on the one before, is intrinsic to the process of learning.

GOOD TEACHERS ARE GOOD MODELS

Students are quick to learn how important principles are by noticing the extent to which their parents and teachers practice what they preach. When adults use organizational and time-management methods effectively, students gain a clearer and stronger picture of what these methods are and are more receptive to mastering them. A teacher who lectures on the importance of developing a logical outline for a term paper but whose presentation is disorganized and unclear is unlikely to be taken seriously by students. The parent who constantly calls attention to the appearance of the child's room but whose own living spaces are cluttered sends a mixed message. Parents who read, write letters, or do other desk work while their children are studying demonstrate the value of language and learning.

Teachers and parents who verbalize their thinking when they solve a problem, apply a process, or learn a skill help children develop and refine their own strategies for learning.

THE STUDENT AND COLLEGE

Before describing some ways in which Landmark College translates the principles we have been discussing into instructional programs and practices for students who learn differently, we will consider some of the special conditions of college attendance in general. College presents new challenges for all students, and these are likely to compound any learning problems the student brings with him.

Most college instructors expect that students come to them equipped to do college-level work. Professors who find their satisfaction in pursuing knowledge and in sharing it may not be prepared to spend time on matters outside their academic disciplines. They as-

sume that students have learned how to study and how
to adapt to varying teaching styles and assignments, and
that if they have not, it is up to them to discover how to
do so on their own.

Many students, some estimate as high as 30 percent, who enter college are unprepared to handle the
special demands of higher education. Their time is
much less structured in college than it was in high
school. When, as is the case in most colleges, classes
meet only three times a week and when students are on
their own to plan their nonclass time, they are often at a
loss. They may put off writing papers and preparing for
exams until the last minute.

All students can become more efficient learners
when they are taught how to study and how to manage
time, but students with a history of school problems
need direct instruction in these areas in order to succeed. While some elementary and secondary schools
offer instruction in study skills, they are often taught in
isolation, and there may be little follow-up to determine
how well students are applying them. For students to
master study skills, parents and teachers must take
them seriously. They must be willing to spend enough
time, they must be patient, and they must be consistent.
Nicole commented toward the end of the summer program at Landmark College, "I've been in study-skills
programs all my life. None of them worked. The difference here is that the focus is on finding out how you
learn and then giving you the tools that work best for
you." Another student remarked after completing the
study-skills program, "There is no reason that anyone
should have to come to this campus. Everything we are
taught here could be taught much earlier."

Learning how to study, to organize, and to manage

time opens the doors for filling in gaps in academic content and provides a solid foundation for future study and work. These skills, as we have seen, often must be taught directly, particularly when students have a history of difficulty in school. For these reasons, all Landmark College students take a study-skills course either in the summer program or in the first semester of the regular school year.

THE MASTER NOTEBOOK

One of the central elements of this study-skills course is the Master Notebook system, which provides instruction in note taking, revising lecture and reading notes, and summarizing information daily and weekly. Although the Master Notebook system was developed for use with college students, it has been successfully adapted for use in middle and high schools. At Landmark, students have a Master Notebook in every course, set up with variations to meet the special requirements of each.

The Notebook consists of a three-ring binder, notebook section dividers, and pockets. Students separate the main part of the notebook into sections labeled to indicate the location of class notes, handouts, weekly lecture-note summaries, tests, and homework. In the left-hand pocket they are instructed to keep planning and organizing materials, such as calendars, appointments, and due dates.

Notebook paper is divided into two columns, with one-third of the page on the left and two-thirds on the right. Students record class notes in the right-hand column of the paper. During class lectures, students are

encouraged to record as many details here as possible
without trying to organize them. In the left-hand column, either in class or within the following twenty-four
hours, they list key words and main ideas.

Students review and revise their notes before they
return to class the next day, using a study process that
reinforces organization and comprehension:

- pull out main ideas and record them in the left-
  hand column of the note page
- highlight important words, phrases, and points
- compare notes with a study partner to fill in
  information gaps
- on the page facing the notes, record questions to
  clarify information, to establish connections
  with prior knowledge, and to anticipate likely
  test questions
- summarize and paraphrase notes
- check comprehension by turning main ideas in
  the left-hand column into questions and answering those questions with the information in the
  right-hand column

Students may be required to submit a summary of
the week's lectures and assigned readings to each instructor, and instructors often evaluate students' notebooks and study procedures.

Checking the study process by reviewing the Notebook is part of diagnostic teaching by instructors. These
checks also help students to discipline themselves to
keep the Notebook current. The Master Notebook is
both a product and a process. Students sometimes complain about this rigorous procedure, but most of them

Master Notebook Study System   pg. 4
Lecture: J. Smith   10/14/93

Need for Study System	-Study system can determine success, esp. in H.S. and college

MNB: Product for organizing information	- MNB: product and process
	- Product: portable filing system and information center
	   - contains all notes, handouts, tests, papers, etc., from course
	   - organized into different sections

Process: Incorporates various study skills	- Process: daily and weekly steps for note taking, note revision, organization, summary writing, studying, test preparation
Instructor: Plays important role in teaching, monitoring	- 4 things instructor can do to assist: 1. Assign students to purchase materials 2. Micro-unit each step 3. Check notebook regularly 4. Give students feedback

TEACHING A STUDY SKILLS SYSTEM THAT WORKS!

come to appreciate its value when they reap its benefits at the end of the semester.

> I've talked to former students now in graduate school who use the two-column note system and are getting better grades than others of equal intelligence in the same class. Furthermore, methods of organization are critical, not only in college, but in life. All these tools work, and we just need to use those that work best for each of us.
>
> Kevin Gott

Inside Landmark College

Now we will take a brief look at how the faculty at Landmark College translate some of the teaching principles discussed above into action.

1. Most readers are familiar with the course syllabus college instructors usually provide, consisting of an outline of the topics to be covered, the readings required, and due dates for assignments. At Landmark College, instructors have expanded the syllabus to be more comprehensive. Each course syllabus spells out in detail the content and expectations with respect to the following:
   - specific course objectives
   - skills to be emphasized and checked periodically
   - important dates, assignments, and deadlines

- grading criteria
- access to the instructor outside of class

A Landmark College course syllabus is comparable to a blueprint for constructing a house: it is detailed, precise, and subject to alteration once the job is begun. When unforeseen conditions force a change in content or quantity of material to be covered, the instructor modifies the syllabus and provides students with the updated version.

2. To set the stage for each day's class, instructors post an agenda, usually written on the chalkboard in a designated spot so students become used to looking for it as they enter the classroom. The instructor allocates a few minutes at the start of class to going over the agenda, which includes the major topics to be covered that day, the ways that these topics will be presented (e.g., lecture, discussion, student paper, debate), and the time planned for each topic. As the class proceeds, the agenda may be modified, or it may serve as a reminder if discussion begins to stray from the listed topics.

3. To introduce a long-term project, instructors may provide "advance organizers," usually in the form of a handout containing these items:

- a unit theme or topic statement with an outline or diagram to support the statement visually
- a description of the unit objectives, often in the form of questions that the unit will address

- a list of key vocabulary and terms
- the steps required to complete the unit

After discussing this advance organizer at the beginning of the unit, the instructor refers to it along with the syllabus and daily agenda until the unit is completed.

4. Landmark College instructors provide for the various learning styles and strengths of their students by using multisensory techniques to present material. Most of these we have discussed extensively in previous sections of the book.
5. Instructors set aside time at the end of each class to summarize, or to have students summarize, a few key topics or concepts presented. In addition, they review short- and long-term assignments, directions, guidelines, and suitable methods for completing these assignments.
6. Instructors check their teaching effectiveness and student progress at frequent intervals through weekly quizzes and summaries, student conferences, and question-and-answer discussion sessions. These often give clues to a student's level of understanding and point out areas where he is having difficulty.
7. Because many students need help learning how to prepare for and take examinations, Landmark instructors give more frequent quizzes and tests. They guide students to form and use study groups to review and rehearse information, teach them how to anticipate test questions, give practice tests, and discuss the ways in which students approached the questions.

Teaching Principles: A Summary

We have discussed what we consider the most important principles of teaching. Parents, teachers, and employers who put these principles into practice are likely to be rewarded by seeing their children, students, and employees gain in knowledge, productivity, and self-respect. To review and summarize, these principles are:

- Make no assumptions about what students know.
- Find point zero and begin instruction there.
- Hold students accountable for what they are capable of doing.
- Use multisensory teaching methods.
- Help students see the rules, patterns, and structure in what they are studying.
- Teach diagnostically, using student errors as a tool for planning instruction.
- Encourage students to analyze their mistakes and learn from them.
- Give the gift of time.
- Break instruction into manageable chunks, or "micro-units."
- Capitalize on student interests and expertise, both academic and nonacademic.
- Teach time management and study skills using a consistent format, such as the Master Notebook.
- Practice essential skills to the point of automatization.

- Establish a strong foundation of skill and knowledge and then spiral upward.
- Seek opportunities to apply skills, information, and concepts to related and different situations.
- Be a model: practice what you are teaching.

7. In the Home

> I began to believe that I was not as smart as the other kids. By some magic that had nothing to do with passing tests, I found myself in the eighth grade. But every day was a battle for me in school then. Every class was a sword that on every passing day cut deeper and left more scars on my mind and heart. Some of you may know similar feelings: ridiculed at school, misunderstood even at home. I knew my parents loved me deeply and were just showing their concern; however, they echoed the message from school: "You're doing everything wrong."
>
> Robert Herman

PARENTS, CHILDREN, AND THE SELF-CONCEPT TRIANGLE

Throughout this book, we have stressed that students learn best when parents, teachers, and students work as a team. Each has a critical part to play in the student's education. When parents view schools and teachers as the sole responsible parties, they lose the opportunity to support their children. Parents can enhance their children's chances for learning success by becoming active in and knowledgeable about the learning process. Then they can more consciously seek to understand their children, to support them when support is needed, and to demonstrate their belief that together they can build a better future.

In the preceding chapters, we discussed ways people learn and problems that can interfere with learning, and we presented some suggestions for parents and teachers to use when dealing with particular types of learning differences. In the chapter on educational assessment, we emphasized how the information produced by testing gives parents and students an understanding of the student's educational needs and how it provides realistic hope for the student's progress. Here we focus more specifically on the important role parents can play in the learning process at home, using many of the same principles and practices discussed earlier.

All parents hold hopes and expectations for their children. The parents we met in Chapter 1 represent the range of experiences and emotions that are common when those hopes and expectations are not realized. Most of the information and the examples we have used up to this point have a direct bearing on school achievement. Parents are the child's first and most important teachers, and there is much that they can do at home to make a real difference in their child's development.

College students with learning problems tell us about ways in which their parents supported them, or, in some cases, made them feel even more isolated. Sandy tells the story of how her parents sent her to a school several counties away from home. They had investigated a special class there and believed that it would be the right place for her. They had met the teacher and felt that he had a good understanding of Sandy's needs. Unfortunately, that teacher left several weeks after Sandy started in his class, and the series of substitute teachers were unable to maintain structure in learning or discipline. Sandy recalls that experience clearly:

> There was one boy who was quiet like me, and the other seven students were always picking on us. I felt intimidated and scared. When I tried to talk to whatever teacher was there, she usually sympathized, but the other kids didn't pay any attention to her. They knew there would be another teacher in a day or so.

When Sandy told her parents what was happening, they took her out of that school and put her in a class in their own district. They made a point of letting her know that no matter what happened in school, they knew she was smart. She was called names at school, however, a practice that Sandy's parents and teachers were only partially successful in confronting and limiting. By the time she reached high school, Sandy spent over half of each day in regular classes. Her parents encouraged her to do her best, but they did not place unrealistic expectations on her. They knew, and they continued to let her know, that she had ability, that it was okay that she learned differently. Through their words and actions, they made it clear that they had faith in her, respected her, and loved her.

THE SELF-CONCEPT TRIANGLE

Even though they probably never thought about it, Sandy's parents instinctively understood what James Baucom, Landmark College's academic dean, calls "The Self-Concept Triangle." The lives of children and high school and college students are chiefly defined by three sets of experiences. The sides of The Self-Concept Triangle represent these three areas: school, social life, and home life. We know that people who feel unworthy or unloved are seldom able to perform effectively. We also know that as long as there is one major aspect in our lives that is affirming, we are better able to overcome negative feelings about ourselves. For children and older students to feel good about themselves, they must have consistent, clear, and positive messages from at least one of the three sides of the triangle.

Sandy went through most of her school years with neutral or negative feedback from the school side. Until she reached high school, her social life was almost non-existent. She had dropped out of after-school activities because she got tired of being teased. She did play in the band, but made few friends until her junior year. It was then that her art teacher selected her to be her assistant and her counselor arranged her schedule so that she could teach some art classes in the middle school. Her sculptures were displayed in the school library, and she won first prize in a citywide art competition. She continued to get C's, with an occasional B, in her academic subjects.

With little support from the school side and not much more from the social side, Sandy was fortunate to

Self-Concept Triangle

have a home side that was so strong. Even though she often felt sad and disappointed that she was not getting better grades, she never doubted that she was intelligent. "No matter how many times I heard the word 'dummy,' " she says, "I knew it didn't apply to me."

Larry's experience was quite different.

> I know that my parents did what they did because they really cared about me. But when I was a kid I thought they just didn't love me. They were always on me, pushing me and punishing me. My father would try to help me with my homework, but he usually got so frustrated that he'd start yelling. I can't tell you how many times he said, "If you'd quit goofing off and just pay attention and try, you could do this work."

Neither the home nor the school side of the Self-Concept Triangle provided much support for Larry. He got the same messages from most of his teachers that he got at home. By the time Larry entered junior high school, he had come to believe that he was never going to please either his parents or his teachers. It is not surprising that he began to seek approval from his classmates, especially those who were, like him, the ones who were not doing well in school.

> I found out that these kids looked up to me when I talked back to the teacher. They were angry and hurt, like me. We skipped school and hung out at the mall. The only times I felt good about myself were when I was with these friends, but we were a bad influence on one another. I was headed for big-time trouble when I got lucky. My gym teacher saw that I was a really good soccer player and talked me into trying out for the team. When I got into soccer, I was successful on the field and I stopped skipping school. We had practices almost every afternoon, so I didn't have time to hang out. Because anyone on a school team had to have passing grades, I began to go to my teachers for extra help. I asked my parents if I could have a tutor. I think that was the happiest day of their lives.

"It surely was," exclaimed Larry's father. Larry's parents commented on their struggles to understand and help him.

> We were so confused and frustrated. We just couldn't seem to get anywhere with him. We had pretty much decided that he just didn't care. We fell right into the trap of blaming him, like parents do when they don't understand their kids.

SUPPORTING YOUR CHILD

When they were asked what message they would like to send to parents, Landmark College students came up with several. No matter how they expressed it, most students agreed that the most important message they wanted parents to hear was "Never give up on your child."

Mary Jo advises parents "to learn how your child learns and provide positive reinforcement whenever you can." Greg says, "A certain amount of pushing is OK, but too much can be bad. Avoid overkill. Be very specific with goals. Never give your child reason to believe that he is not smart."

With sympathetic insight, Betty puts herself in the place of her parents.

> They want to help you and heal you and make it go away. Pick that little thing up [the learning problem] and throw it away. Get a tutor to fix it or a doctor or a psychologist. What they need to do first is help us find out how we learn.

Of all the roles and responsibilities parenthood brings, the most important are loving, understanding, and supporting the child. Parents need to let their child know how much they appreciate him for what he can do, and how much they enjoy and respect his special qualities.

In every parent-child relationship there will be conflicts and misunderstandings, and this is never more likely than when the child runs into obstacles. Often these obstacles occur in school, a crucially important part of his life. Parents then are challenged to expand their understanding and support. Even when the situation appears bleak, they need to encourage the child to see that hope for improvement remains. Parents who place confidence in their children, who believe that they will succeed in the end, and who actively work with them to find the means to do so are building a strong foundation of attitudes and values. These, more than any attempts to give specific help with particular academic problems, will help their children to overcome their difficulties.

MOTIVATION

When children have school problems, it is tempting to blame these problems on a lack of motivation. Parents and teachers often think of motivation as something the child has or lacks as an inherent personality trait.

Motivation depends on several factors: the student's interest and enjoyment in the activity, his understanding of the processes required, and the extent to which his efforts are rewarded by success. When learning experiences result in success that the student can attribute to his own efforts and abilities, his motivation increases. On the other hand, if he feels that his efforts do not affect the outcome of the activity or assignment, his motivation to repeat the same or similar task is diminished. As Phil recounts:

> During my early school years, I started out each year all gung-ho. Hoping to succeed, I put my best effort into studying and paying attention in class. But before long, each year, the work got harder. By the time we got grades, I usually was failing at least half of my classes. From things that were said to me, I got the feeling that everyone thought I was a lazy troublemaker. After a while, I began to believe that picture. Then, frustrated and angry, I'd say to myself, "Hey, I can get this label with hardly any effort." And minimal effort is what I produced the rest of the year.

The experiences of Sandy, Larry, Mary Jo, Betty, Greg, and Phil remind us how important it is for parents to work with their children, helping them to analyze learning situations that are frustrating and unsuccessful and to determine what they can do to improve the situation.

Even the most frustrating situations usually have some bright spots for which parents can honestly praise their children. Pointing out a specific area of improvement in an otherwise unsuccessful assignment pays greater long-term dividends than paying attention only to errors or criticizing children for lack of motivation. Saving early assignments in a folder and bringing them out at a later date so the child can see how much he has improved, even when his current assignment is flawed, is an effective way to demonstrate that continued effort makes sense.

Children who do poorly in school are often told they would be more successful if they were motivated, but the reverse is usually the case: Most children would be more motivated if they experienced more successes that they could attribute to their own efforts.

SUCCESSFUL PARENTS/STRUGGLING CHILDREN

Quite often the parents of children who struggle to learn are, themselves, successful. Whether or not parents hold their own experiences as models for their children, the fact that they are successful adults may send powerful messages to the child. These messages may be either positive or negative. While children often share the same learning styles as one or both of their parents, there are numerous cases where at least one parent finds it difficult to understand why a child is having trouble in school. This parent may send the message that if only the child would try harder, he could be successful. Some parents may have forgotten how much of their success they owe to a teacher or mentor who gave them the encouragement and understanding they needed when they needed it most.

Parents who hope to see their children experience the satisfactions they enjoy can set the stage best by helping them to understand that successful people are those who have learned to handle frustrations, setbacks, and self-doubt. They can share experiences from their own lives and those of other successful people to show the importance of problem-solving techniques and of changing perspectives in dealing effectively with difficulties. Parents who model and coach, rather than preach, help their children analyze difficulties and learn effective means for solving problems.

D.J. reports that one of the things that has helped

him the most is that his father has shared with him the fact that he, too, had problems in school. Because his father is a successful small businessman, this sharing gave D.J. new confidence in himself.

> Before I knew that Dad had struggled so hard in school, I just figured that there was something wrong with me. When he told me about his experiences in school, they were just like what I was having. So this lightbulb went off in my head: "If Dad came out of this okay, I can, too."

PRAISE AND SELF-ESTEEM

Confidence and feelings of self-worth grow from real, tangible successes, not from hollow praise. With the best of intentions, parents and teachers may try to support the child's self-esteem by giving unqualified or unearned praise. While everyone may at times need such praise, most are quick to recognize whether it is deserved.

Children know when their efforts have been inadequate or their accomplishments minimal. When they have been, children may see unjustified praise as condescending or as an indication that teachers or parents hold low expectations for their performance. On the other hand, if children receive and accept as their due exaggerated praise, they may develop a distorted sense of their skills. They are then vulnerable to greater disappointments when they realize that they have been living with a inflated image of themselves. The parent who wants to foster self-esteem needs to set realistic expectations for his child and to confront problems honestly. In doing so, he can still find many reasons to praise the child. While good grades, test results, and awards are worthy of parental recognition, the basic attitudes and traits that can lead to long-term success are even more praiseworthy. Hard work, regular attendance, persistence, willingness to seek help, and accepting and learning from mistakes are some of the best reasons for parents to praise their children. Praising the child's efforts supports the development of motivation as well.

SUPPORTING PASSIONATE INTERESTS

Parents can foster learning by looking for and encouraging their child's special interests. Being successful and recognized for our success is one of the chief ways we come to like and respect ourselves, no matter how old we are. For children and young adults, being acknowledged for doing well in a specific area can be a powerful motivator for continuing to try in school. It was his success at soccer that prompted Larry on page 200 to alter his attitude about school. Students who continue to strive despite difficulties often do so because there is something in their lives that is affirming, that makes them feel good about themselves, that renews their energy, and that stimulates their thoughts.

The support a student gets from his parents as he works toward success in school constitutes one side, and a potent one, of the Self-Concept Triangle. It can become even stronger and more influential when the student is engaged in activities that hold real appeal for him. These activities may be broad in scope (such as sports, drama, music, or public service) or more focused (such as cartooning, card collecting, or becoming an expert on frogs of the rain forest). Given the chance to excel in something that excites him does more than simply offset the frustration his school problems may create. When engaged in an activity he loves, he draws on and develops his strengths, uses and improves skills that support his interest, and obtains satisfaction from his successes. Among the lifelong skills and attitudes he is likely to acquire in this way are these:

- systematically setting goals
- gathering and organizing information
- listening carefully and communicating clearly
- solving problems
- making choices and decisions
- accepting responsibility
- discovering that learning and work can be fun

Students who develop an area of expertise are likely to have more opportunities to become leaders, to earn the respect of others, and to develop social connections and relationships around those interests. They will be able to draw upon the skills and knowledge they develop in these activities and apply them in other activities, both academic and nonacademic.

ORGANIZATION IN THE HOME

Equally important in the home as in school and on the job, organization can make the difference between a smooth and generally happy situation and one that is plagued by argument, disorder, and failure to complete tasks. We have seen in previous chapters that students who learn to plan and organize their time and materials have a better chance to succeed in school.

A good place to examine organization in the home is by looking at the habits and routines that contribute to the daily activities of the family. Too often when we think of habits, we think first of "bad habits" or "mindless habits," as those things we ought to "kick." However, habits and routines are important to a smoothly running home because they are skills we have largely automatized, skills that demand little thought, attention, or memory. We can focus our efforts elsewhere when we rely on a foundation of good habits.

To promote improved organization in the home, parents can start by recognizing the good habits and routines that already exist, refining them to reflect the family's current needs. Here are some typical family habits and routines that can help:

1. Set up a bulletin board with a large master calendar in a place where everyone will see it each day. The daily spaces should be large enough for recording appointments, activities, and reminders, and for listing the names of the individuals involved. Using a color code to identify each member of the family can make the calendar easier to scan, if necessary. Older children can be responsible for recording their activities and relevant information on the calendar. Teenagers with demanding academic and social schedules may need to carry a personal calendar as well. Parents can help them start this good habit by providing an appointment book and checking with them from time to time to see that

they are keeping it up to date and consistent with the master calendar. The bulletin board is also a good place to tack tickets, directions, invitations, and receipts so they can be located readily when needed.

2. Post daily and weekly chores in a prominent place, such as the refrigerator door. If family members perform their assigned chores regularly over a period of time, they will begin to become routine. Young children—and older children with attention, memory, and organization problems—may need to have the day, time, and nature of each chore specified (Bob: Monday, Wednesday, Friday morning before school, put in a load of laundry). Every family member can share in the household responsibilities when they are clearly stated and are appropriate to the age and ability of each. Everyone should know in advance the consequences of failing to perform their duties.

3. Maintain "To Do" and "To Buy" lists on the refrigerator, by the telephone, or in some equally accessible place. If Dad finishes off the duct tape, Sis notices that the faucet in the bathtub is leaking, or Bob opens up the last jar of mustard, they should know where to record that information so that the household inventory and the odd-jobs needs are plain to see. These lists save time when parents shop or arrange for repairs, and the entire family shares in the responsibility for remembering what needs to be done. When this habit is established, children know where they can record their needs ("Mom, I need a protractor for math by next week").

4. Set up specific locations for items that family members use or refer to frequently—mittens, the back door key, lunch money, school notices, for example. Organize in the same spot or container items that are used together, such as a soccer bag or a library book tote. Even young children can participate productively in placing materials where they belong when there is an explicit system in place—hanging up the tools in the garage according to their shapes or sorting silverware into a tray—and in doing so they form good habits for later life.

5. Develop routines that your child can master and take over (like laying out school clothes the night before or packing up the school backpack after homework is done) that will address problem areas such as getting ready and finding materials on school mornings.

6. Family members can work together, combining routines with pleasurable activities. One family watches TV together every Sunday night and at the same time sorts and folds laundry. Another puts on loud, fast music every Saturday morning while they spend an hour cleaning the house.

As families work to improve organization in the home, they need to remember that having family fun is important, sometimes even more important than cleaning the garage. So work on planning, but be flexible. Learn to distinguish tasks that absolutely must be completed by a certain date (paying the rent or taxes) and those that can be postponed without creating a problem (washing the car).

Busy parents may view these suggestions as unrealistic, feeling that there is no way they can fit them into an already overloaded schedule. Perhaps the list will serve as a springboard to altering some household activities in ways that are realistic for the particular circumstances in the home. Whatever those may be, we encourage parents to experiment with suggestions that seem reasonable to them.

HOMEWORK

Nowhere are the rewards for establishing habits and routines greater than in the area of homework. Parents can help children develop these habits by setting a regular time for doing homework, a time that takes into account the child's need to have a break from schoolwork and the importance of getting work done early in the evening. For many students the time that serves both of these purposes is right after dinner. Students usually can concentrate best in a place that is well lit and large enough to accommodate all the books and materials they need to complete assignments, without being distracted (away from the telephone, TV, and Internet).

School districts vary in their policies regarding homework, and parents should familiarize themselves with those policies. We believe that all children, especially those with learning problems, can profit from thoughtful homework assignments and that they should be given such assignments regularly not later than the upper elementary grades. If district policy does not require this practice, parents may be able to request homework, based on the premise that appropriate assignments will help to reinforce what students are expected to master in class.

Whether or not parents should help with homework and if they do what kinds of help are appropriate
are concerns that every family faces. In the best of all
possible worlds, all teachers would give for homework
only assignments that reinforce the material and the
skills they have taught and for which the students have
demonstrated enough mastery to proceed independently. In the real world, however, students often have
assignments that call for self-teaching or assume a mastery level they do not have. When parents discuss assignments and work with their child, they gain a good
sense of what he can do independently and what
problems he is encountering. This understanding, in
turn, forms the basis for constructive discussions with
teachers and óther school personnel.

In many families, homework develops into a sore
spot. Here are some typical reasons why children have
trouble with their homework:

- **The student lacks the basic skills required to
  do the assignment.** Sometimes, assignments assume that the student has mastered a skill when,
  in fact, he has not. As a result, he may spend
  most of his homework time struggling with the
  skill involved and thus be unable to pay sufficient attention to the substance of the assignment. An example of this is an assignment that
  requires the student to prepare written answers
  to questions about a short story. The purpose of
  the assignment is to see how well the student
  understands the story and to encourage critical
  thinking. But the student who has not mastered
  the skills of spelling words or writing complete
  sentences may not be able to complete the as-

signment, even though he could easily demonstrate (by answering questions orally) that he
comprehends the story and has thought about it
critically.

- **The student is required to apply new information that he does not yet fully understand.** Math
and science assignments in particular may require the student to apply formulas or carry out
procedures that he has been introduced to but
does not yet comprehend. Or as he attempts to
complete an assignment involving long division,
for example, his lack of understanding may lead
him to practice incorrectly. Repeatedly practicing in this way may fix in his memory a flawed
procedure, which later must be removed and re-
placed by the correct one.
- **The student may be able to do the work but finds
the volume of work assigned too great.** Although
many students have trouble with long assignments, this is a particular area of difficulty for
students who process information slowly, or
who have trouble expressing themselves in writing. They can be overwhelmed by assignments
that include numerous questions or problems, or
extend over long periods of time.
- **The student may have trouble following directions or have difficulty understanding the assignment.** Students may be unable to begin an
assignment, even if the work otherwise makes
reasonable demands on their skills. Students
who have trouble following clear directions may
be hopelessly lost if directions are not clear.
- **The student may be disorganized with his assignments and materials.** Students who have

trouble keeping track of assignments and locating and bringing home the necessary materials
will be unable to complete their homework successfully.

Before parents start to help with homework, it is
important for them to remember that they should provide help that addresses "weak links" in their child's
performance and that they should not do things the
child is capable of doing himself. Children generally
resent being supervised or helped in areas where they
are competent. Appropriate help with homework starts
with careful observations.

When you have a good idea why your child is having such a hard time with homework, speak with his
teacher, describing what you have observed as specifically as possible. As with any school-related problem,
the ideal approach is a team approach in which the
student, teacher, and parent work together to find a
solution. The potential for the parent and child to get in
battles over homework is minimized when the parent is
part of a team and has a defined role that the child
understands.

Conditions such as large class sizes and diminish-
ing resources, over which teachers have no control,
make it difficult for them to give individualized homework assignments. Most teachers are able and willing to
make adjustments in assignments for students with
learning differences. But no matter how well teachers
prepare and present homework assignments, how much
consideration they give to the individual learning levels
and needs of their students, or how open they are to
modifying their requirements, the burden of responsibility for homework remains with the student and the

home. Therefore, the more practical concrete ways parents can support their children, the better able they will be to meet this responsibility.

Here are some guidelines you may find useful whether you are working alone or as part of a team:

- Identify the parts of the assignment that cause the most difficulty and address them specifically.

  1. Coach the student who has trouble paying attention or following directions at the beginning and ending stages of the assignment, and if the assignment runs over a period of time, at checkpoints along the way.
  2. Be available to spell words for a child who has not made spelling and the mechanics of writing automatic, so that he can maintain the flow of his thoughts while he writes.
  3. If your child has weak fine motor control, which interferes with his handwriting, consider serving as his secretary for one section of a long writing assignment by recording, for example, the ideas he comes up with in a brainstorming session.

- If his problems are the result of poor skills (for example, lack of mastery of the multiplication table or of spelling rules), ask if his teacher can send home individualized regular practice in these areas. Students who do not master basic skills in elementary school seldom get additional practice in secondary school. With guidance from teachers, you can engage your child in the frequent short practice sessions he needs to be successful.

- If your child consistently has difficulty understanding the content and concepts in his assignments, notify his teacher promptly. Perhaps he needs accommodations, such as extended time to complete work, academic support from a school specialist, or tutoring. Without appropriate help, this child runs the risk of getting so far behind his classmates that it will be almost impossible for him to catch up.

- If your child frequently is unable to complete all his assignments when they are due, keep track of how much time he spends on each of them. Try to determine whether one specific subject is particularly troublesome or whether the problem is more generalized. Check with his teachers to see if they are willing to adjust the amount of homework given (for example, assigning fifteen rather than thirty long-division problems) or to limit the time he spends on any particular subject.

- Particularly if organization is a problem for the student, help him to learn his role in homework completion.

  1. Encourage him to copy assignments for each class legibly in an organized form in an assignment notebook.
  2. Get him in the habit of seeking clarification from the teacher if he is unsure of an assignment. This could involve a regular check-in with the teacher about the assignment at the close of each class.
  3. Guide him to accept responsibility for putting the assignment notebook in a book bag or

backpack that he carries back and forth from school every day.

4. Encourage him to set aside a short time at the end of the school day to review his assignments and check to see that he has the required materials.

- If your child cannot sustain attention and work independently, establish a schedule that includes the time he must work on his own before asking for help or includes times when you will be available to help him. By asking him about his assignments before he begins to work, you can determine whether or not he understands what he is supposed to do. Discuss with him the kinds of help you will give him and the things you expect him to do on his own. It is also a good idea to schedule some breaks and to limit the number of times he spontaneously interrupts himself ("I've got to get a drink," "I just have to call Dave and ask him how much he has finished").

- Show by your actions that you value good work habits. If you can, spend time reading or doing desk work while your child is doing homework.

There are many possible variations in the ways parents can provide positive support for their children in the area of homework. Perhaps the most important things to do are these:

- Be interested and let your child know you value his work.
- Be supportive without taking over and doing the work yourself.

- Be attentive to the time he is spending and to the problems he encounters.
- Be prepared to discuss problems with his teachers by observing where he has difficulty. Be as specific as possible when you meet his teachers. Reporting that he is spending three hours each night on his math homework indicates something is wrong, but being able to pinpoint where he has most trouble ("He seems to get bogged down every time he has to solve word problems that involve time") can alert his teacher to the probable cause.
- Create a positive climate for homework completion. Seek help from teachers or counselors if homework develops into a battle.

PROMOTING LANGUAGE SKILLS AT HOME

In Chapter 2 we described the ways children acquire language. We noted that children whose homes are rich in language experiences have a strong foundation for understanding and learning in school. Some language principles parents can employ with their children are these:

- Allowing time for the child to finish his sentences, rather than letting others—or his facial or body expressions—speak for him.
- Providing many opportunities for the child to grasp the language of sequencing and organizing. Using words like "first," "next," "then," and "finally" in telling stories or giving directions helps to order and structure everyday events.
- Talking to the child, reading to him, and asking him questions and listening carefully to his an-

swers, are simple but effective methods of helping him to gain control of language.

- Responding to the child's questions and comments and praising him whenever possible for
his use of language and the ideas he expresses.

For further ideas and activities, review pages 61 and
68–70 in Chapter 2.

RECORD KEEPING

Throughout this book, we have emphasized how important organizational skills and strategies are in supporting understanding and learning, and we have used the
example of the Master Notebook. Many children enjoy
collecting and reviewing their schoolwork, art projects,
and other achievements in a scrapbook or file. When a
child runs into difficulty in school, a more systematic
approach may be needed. Parents can adapt and keep a
Master Notebook to organize important materials that
reflect the student's patterns of learning and achievement and his overall progress. Information contained in
the notebook can be organized by topic, separated into
sections, and arranged according to date, usually with
the most recent date appearing first. The notebook
might include sections for the following records:

- report cards, grades, teacher comments, and
school transcripts
- copies of formal assessments and other reports
from specialists
- educational plans developed by the student's
team, including changes made in those plans

- correspondence to and from school personnel and others involved in evaluating, planning, or working with the student
- summaries of all conferences, telephone conversations, and meetings, their dates, the names of participants, and the agreements reached, including who agreed to do what and by what date
- newspaper and magazine articles and readings
- lists of organizations and related resources, with names, telephone numbers, and addresses

This record—along with a portfolio of work samples from the beginning, middle, and end of each school year—will document the student's progress in a systematic, orderly, and meaningful way.

GATHERING INFORMATION

If your child has a learning disability, an important step in getting him help is to learn as much as possible about it. In recent years many useful articles and books by parents, teachers, learning-disabilities specialists, and learning-disabled individuals themselves have been written. (Some of those we have found most helpful are listed in Appendix D and Appendix E, beginning on page 253.) The local librarian can help you find these, as well as a number of newspaper and magazine articles. The Internet is an increasingly valuable resource. In most states and many communities, there are chapters of national organizations that assist parents, teachers, and students in understanding learning difficulties. Several of these are listed in Appendix C. Parents often find that sharing their concerns with other parents

whose children have learning problems is both practical and helpful. Usually a parent who has dealt with
similar problems in the same school is willing to help
others who are exploring these problems for the first
time. You can also learn a great deal by sitting in on your
child's classes and seeing the ways he functions in that
setting.

The better informed you are, the better able you
will be to engage in productive meetings with your
child's teachers. Potentially, they are the single most
important source of information about his academic
performance, behavior, and learning needs. For parent-
teacher meetings to serve the child well, those participating should prepare for them consciously, reviewing
concerns, noting questions, and being ready to listen
and to offer suggestions. All should enter these meetings expecting the other participants to be sincere in
their desire to find answers. Parents and teachers see the
child in different environments and may find the picture the other presents hard to accept. Sometimes parents may question whether school personnel are trying
to understand and help their child. When this happens,
parents may decide to make demands accompanied by
threats and to carry them to increasingly higher levels in
the school system and even to the courts. When all other
avenues have been explored and the child's needs re-
main unaddressed, taking strong action may be necessary. That, however, is not the place to start. Many cases
that reach boards of arbitration or the courts might be
avoided if each party believed that the other was prepared to spend the necessary time and give the necessary thought to finding common ground.

At all meetings, but especially at the first one, parents should resist coming to conclusions or flatly reject-

ing or accepting the teacher's judgments and recommendations. Conference participants should try to focus their attention on what is actually occurring, not on what they think is causing the problem.

Frequently, those at such meetings decide that before they make any decisions about the child's school program, the child should undergo a thorough assessment. Chapter 5 details that process and describes ways to get the most from diagnostic testing. Following this, the next step is for parents and school personnel to meet (along with the student himself whenever appropriate) to review the evaluation and to create an educational program that reflects the diagnostic findings. State and federal laws require schools to invite parents as full participants in planning their child's education. This is both a right and a responsibility that parents are encouraged to take seriously. As we have said numerous times, the prospects for academic achievement are strengthened when teachers, parents, and students respect one another and contribute to a continuing team approach for solving problems.

DEVELOPING EDUCATIONAL PROGRAMS

Once team members agree on an educational program, their responsibilities are just beginning. Over the years, this program will have to be adjusted many times. As he advances from grade to grade, the child also undergoes physical and emotional changes that may affect his academic life. A plan that works well in third grade is seldom as effective in seventh grade. Parents usually are sensitive to changes, both subtle and obvious, in their children, although they sometimes do not understand

the causes. A previously docile child may become re-
bellious or remote as he enters adolescence; the child
who loved to read but hated to write may turn against
reading in junior high school.

Most children, not only those with learning problems, find that changes in curricula during certain years
bring new expectations and demands. In any of the
transition grades (typically, grades three, six, nine, and
twelve), students may for the first time run into obstacles. At these grades, students are expected to take on
larger amounts of work; they are expected to be able to
read independently, to write effectively, to organize
their work, and to manage their time at levels significantly higher than those expected in the preceding
grade. When students reach one of these transition periods, parents should recognize that the workload and
expectations are more demanding and that changes in
the educational program may be needed.

Conclusion

There are so many ways parents can help to build a
strong side on the child's Self-Concept Triangle and, at
the same time, encourage and support him as he faces
new experiences and challenges in school and in the
community. We have made many suggestions arising
from our experiences with students, knowing that you
will find other ways that will work well for you.

Above all, no matter how rough things may get for
you and for your child, remember that you, like all
parents, have to learn the business of being parents on

the job. You will make mistakes, you will feel anger and
sorrow and guilt; all parents do, not just the parents of
children with learning problems. Take time to congratu-
late yourself on the positive steps you have taken, like
putting aside time to learn more about learning and
about ways to help your child. Remember the hours you
have willingly spent patiently supporting him as he
struggled with some aspect of learning. And most of all,
remember that your love, understanding, and hope are
the most important gifts you can give to your child.
With these, and with the wisdom of your experiences,
your child can set his feet firmly on the path to independence.

8. The Independent Learner

> All my life it seemed like I was beating my head against a wall. That wall was the barrier between what I know and my ability to use my knowledge. What I have learned [by learning how I learn] is where the doors are in that wall and how to open them.
>
> Raymond

Education in its broadest sense involves parents, teachers, the community, and the learner in a cooperative, coordinated effort. When students understand how they learn, when they are provided with instruction that makes no assumptions about the level of their knowledge and skills but locates that level and begins instruction there, they are on the road to becoming independent lifelong learners.

Jerome Bruner, a Harvard psychologist who was influential in getting scholars to think about the learning process, claims that any intellectually sound material, no matter how complex, can be taught at the level of a person's ability to understand. Good teachers have always known this. They use their knowledge of their students' backgrounds and abilities and mold their instruction to begin where the students are and move them to the next higher level. In doing so, they may simplify the language of those in the field, and they may make use of events and situations familiar to their students. What they will not do is water-down material so that it becomes less than the truth as it is known by the educated and experienced.

You have been introduced to the process of learning, the variations in the ways children learn, and the ways parents and teachers can support the efforts of those students who learn in nontraditional ways. In presenting this material, we have attempted to take some sophisticated and technical ideas and concepts and relate them to situations familiar to most people. If you have a new understanding of how each of us learns, about the diversity in useful methods of learning, about the multiple intelligences that contribute to individual growth, then we have helped you establish a base for your understanding. Some of you will want to pursue these ideas further, and for that we provide (in Appendix E) a sampling of books that will reinforce and build on those ideas.

Similarly, the material presented here can be simplified and presented to students as early as in elementary school. If all students, whether they learn traditionally or not, are given an opportunity to learn about how they learn, both they and their teachers and parents can avoid some of the pitfalls that befell some of the students we have discussed, and just as important, may gain hope through examples of successes. Those who can tell and demonstrate to others how they learn gain in confidence and achievement. The student who has figured out that he retains information best when he sees, hears, and discusses it can develop and use multi-sensory techniques on his own, becoming increasingly independent in his learning.

A college student, Maria, comments about the power she gained from understanding how she learns.

> I learn best by going beyond the facts and information presented and asking questions to determine the reason and logic behind this material. Once I understand the basis of the knowledge, I can retain it, I can analyze my mistakes, and I feel confident in my ability to use what I have learned as the basis for future learning.

Many adults, without consciously thinking about it, have gained from experience a general sense of how they learn best. On the computer exercise on pages 23–24, most readers probably picked out the approach they would take fairly quickly. The advantage that a student like Maria has over other students who have had few if any learning problems is that she has been compelled by what we call a "disability" to think long, hard, and seriously about how her mind works, about the ways in which she is best able to absorb and retain information.

The ability to think about how we think, to use our minds to help us understand how our minds work, is called **metacognition**. Maria demonstrates that her thinking has matured to this level. As a result, she is well positioned to make maximum use of the mental powers she has. No matter how intelligent or educated a person may be, she will be freed to think and achieve more productively and efficiently if she becomes meta-cognitive.

Maria describes metacognition as a continuous process that is often difficult. It is a process that she believes requires consistent direction and support from parents and teachers:

> It challenges your weaknesses and forces you to look for the light at the end of the tunnel, and if you don't see the light, you have to keep pushing ahead until you do. And when you do see that light, everything that was hidden and even frightening before becomes clear. You know then that no matter how hard things may be in the future, that you have the tools to tackle them, that even when the light may flicker or even disappear, it is still there and you will be able to find it again.

This is the strength that comes from self-knowledge, discovered by a student who reached her late teens with a history of academic failure and low self-esteem. Maria consciously has given great effort to overcoming these problems, and she recognizes that she will have to continue to do so throughout life. But with her understanding of how she learns, she is willing to meet those challenges with hard work. Consider, then, the giant steps that all children and adults could make if they, too, had the opportunity to obtain more than an inkling of how they can make the best possible use of their minds.

With the power this knowledge brings, learners of all ages can begin to advocate for themselves. Students with diagnosed learning problems may require some special modifications as they continue through school and out into the workplace. The challenges of requesting such accommodations are several:

- The person requesting accommodations should have a clear sense of what he truly needs, based on an accurate understanding of his learning strengths and weaknesses.
- He should request those accommodations knowing that he is not asking for special treatment, but rather equal opportunity to learn.
- He should request only those accommodations he truly needs, not everything that is available.
- He should ask for help in a manner that paves the way for others who come behind him.
- He should know his rights and what recourse is available to him if difficulties arise in the process.
- He should not use his difficulties as an excuse.

A group of Landmark College students address this issue thoughtfully in the *New England Postsecondary Consortium on Learning Disabilities Handbook*. In the chapter they wrote for this monograph, they give entering college students with learning problems the benefit of their experience. Their recommendations for ways students who learn differently can become independent self-advocates demonstrate a realistic maturity and thoughtfulness.

(The following section was written by Maryam Ansari, Ron Dantin, Stephanie Ghelman, Elizabeth Horton, Dana Schulte, Nathan Tessmann, and Beth Walsh, students at Landmark College in Putney, Vermont.)

Your most important advocate is yourself. You have to be willing to help yourself if you want help from others. No one is going to help a student who sits back and does nothing. To be an effective self-advocate, here are some things you need to do:

- Understand the nature of your learning disability—not just generally, but specifically. Have documentation on hand that explains your learning disability.
- Understand what modifications or academic adjustments you need in order to learn. Provide documentation for these also.
- Be able to explain your learning disability and your academic needs in a clear and convincing manner. Be specific. Don't expect teachers to understand what your learning disability entails automatically, any more than they should expect their students to grasp a concept the first time around.
- Be assertive, but polite. Never approach your instructors or advisers with an argumentative tone. This could hinder your chances of getting the help you need. Show how willing you are to work with faculty for help and support, keep an open mind about their suggestions, and apply yourself fervently to your work and studies.
- Be confident in the knowledge that you were accepted by your college and considered to be qualified for its academic program. Remember that self-advocacy also means working toward the goal of self-sufficiency. Know what your problems are, but also what the solutions are.

As students leave school or college and enter the workplace, those who have learned responsible self-advocacy can make important contributions in many fields. A former Landmark College student, Chris Tasik, who has worked for several years for a cable TV company, has made the transition from student to employee well. He says:

> Self-advocacy is the scariest part of being a person who learns differently. In the workplace, you need to tie your learning differences to the goals of the business. Showing employers films that focus on the pain and confusion of the learning-disabled only turns them off. You need to put a positive spin on your learning style and those of your coworkers: no sour grapes, no playing the victim. Recently my company held a series of meetings to develop goals for improving our business. I used these goals, along with a videotape, to illustrate the creativity and possibility provided by people who think, learn, and approach tasks differently. All through the presentation I tried to tie this to specific goals the company is working toward.

As a mature adult, Chris does not feel like a victim. But the pain that he and many students have suffered because of their difficulties in school is real. The students we have met in this book have had experiences shared by thousands of others who learn differently.

As we have seen throughout this book, parents and teachers can do much to help children become successful, effective, lifelong learners. The rewards, both to the students and to the parents and teachers who help them, can be enormous.

Those who work with and listen to these students hear, through their voices, a call for changes in the way we understand, support, and teach them. As we recognize the diversity of their needs and talents, we are forced to acknowledge that many of their "problems" are due to our fixed perceptions about how students should learn.

Children with learning problems demand the best of their parents and teachers. To accept the challenge these students offer us, we must respond to their diversity by providing each of them with the experiences and tools he needs to find success. To offer help to a child, we must become lifelong learners ourselves, and develop approaches and techniques based on the new perspectives that each child presents to us. In many ways, we can learn as much from our children as we can teach them.

A wholehearted commitment to their success involves acting on the belief that when they fail, we all fail. We must acknowledge the enormity of the loss when young people whose intelligence, creativity, and problem-solving abilities could make contributions to society give up, drop out, or function significantly below the level they are capable of achieving. We must be willing to examine the practices that have condemned far too many able students to years of unproductive and even damaging experiences.

As parents and teachers, we cannot continue to misunderstand or ignore those who learn differently. We must begin deliberations about effective teaching by examining the richness of variations in learning and by insisting that we provide many pathways to success. We must develop partnerships for learning that include parents, teachers, and students who understand and have common goals.

With our understanding and support, we will see our children become not only independent, but interdependent, compassionate and committed to making the changes that will endow the future, both for themselves and others, with the bright light of hope.

Landmark College: Education Principles in Practice

> Here I experienced academic success for the first time. Here I have learned the skills to manage my work and to produce each and every day, a fact that often amazes me, since it is not consistent with my former leanings toward sabotage and copping out. Most important, it is here that I realized that my instructors are not my enemies. They stressed attitudes toward the world and toward learning that put a kink in my conditioning, forcing me to change the way I view those around me. Through their support and patience I have come to support and be patient with myself.
>
> Jennifer May,
> *Convocation Speech*

> Remember to respect people for what they are, for what they can become, and for the struggle it takes to make that change.
>
> Jim Olivier,
> *Founding President, Landmark College*

In this book we have drawn heavily on examples from Landmark College. There are many fine schools, public and private, that have excellent programs for children who learn differently. Federal and state laws require schools and colleges to accommodate the needs of students with diagnosed learning problems. In the resource list at the end of the book (Appendix B), we provide the names of several sources of information about schools and colleges that serve the learning needs of these students. This list and other resources can also be found on Landmark College's Home Page on the Internet (http://www.landmarkcollege.org).

Landmark College is unique, however, in being the only fully accredited institution of higher education founded specifically for these students. Since its founding in 1985, Landmark College has enrolled more than 1,700 students. All students who attend Landmark share a history of academic problems. They may have been diagnosed as learning disabled or dyslexic or as having an attention disorder. Many have endured years of failure and frustration, and they often doubt their own ability to succeed. Others first encountered academic difficulties when they reached college or graduate school.

Landmark College embodies the conviction of its founder, Charles Drake: With instruction that respects their individual learning needs, its students can learn the language and academic skills they find difficult. He recognized that for some students reaching academic success is very demanding. But Dr. Drake—whose innovative thinking has inspired several generations of students, parents, and educators—understood the factors that would provide the starting point for good teaching and successful learning:

- instruction based on sound teaching principles and tailored to the needs of each student

- instruction that starts at the level where the student's understanding begins to break down
- instruction that guides students step by step to achieve challenging goals
- instruction that encourages the student to discover and to understand the ways in which he learns best and to apply this knowledge
- the student's willingness to accept the discipline of hard work

LANDMARK COLLEGE PRINCIPLES

Landmark College's philosophy consists of a set of principles so simple and clear that many educators agree they should govern good instruction for all students. These principles guide the wide array of specific methods used to help Landmark students achieve success. By applying these principles and implementing these strategies, Landmark College has succeeded in helping students make academic gains and transform their lives.

From the time the college opened its doors to students, these principles have been applied to every issue. As the college has grown, these same principles have guided the expansion and refinement of its programs. By keeping them constantly in mind, the college has retained a strong commitment to its special mission.

Putting the Student Learning at the Center of Education

First, and most important, Landmark College focuses on each student as an individual and measures its success by the progress each makes. Whether considering a new course syllabus, a modification in residence requirements, or a refinement in the disciplinary code, the critical question always is "How will this improve student learning?"

If a student at Landmark has trouble learning, instructors and professors first question whether there is another more effective way to teach him. Faculty recognize that they play a vital role in each student's performance, and they design their teaching to address the student's learning needs. As a result, Landmark faculty have developed a number of innovative teaching methods, educational materials, and curriculum designs.

Developing Skills, Not Bypass Techniques

At Landmark, a major focus of instruction is ensuring that all students master the skills needed to succeed in school and beyond. It is not lack of intelligence but inadequate mastery of skills that has kept many Landmark students from being more successful in their previous schools and colleges.

Some students have used "bypass techniques" in schools and colleges in an effort to compensate for these poor skills. For example, a poor reader may be permitted to use audiotapes of textbooks or be assigned a reader to present text material or examination questions to him orally. Perhaps he is assigned a "designated note taker" or given the option of taking exams orally rather than having to write his responses. Practices such as these are called bypass techniques. Rather than being required to use the skill involved, the student bypasses that skill by some external means. This may enable him to absorb the content of instruction or to express his understanding of it without depending on his reading and writing skills. In many cases, bypass techniques are essential if the student is to keep up with his classmates.

Landmark, however, believes that its students can master the skills they find difficult and leave bypassing behind them. Capitalizing on their strengths, students learn, to the level of their potential, to read efficiently and with comprehension, to write clearly, to organize their work, and to use study time effectively. Consistent with its belief that its students can learn, Landmark designs instruction in basic language and learning skills to move the student beyond dependence. The goal is to develop lifelong learners.

Landmark College rejects the notion that skills instruction and college education are incompatible. Much of what colleges have always taught depends on skills. Writing an effective brief in law school integrates a number of sophisticated, finely tuned skills, skills that most students learn best when they are taught them directly. Skills instruction is not limited to the "3 R's." It is fundamental at all levels of education, from kindergarten through professional schools.

Starting Where Understanding Breaks Down

In planning for a student's instruction in any subject, the first step is to find out what he has mastered and at what point his understanding breaks down. Older students often welcome the opportunity to work on basic skills. Dan Munley, a twenty-seven-year-old, had managed to get through college and into law school despite a long history of poor organizational skills. "Both my parents and I just figured I was lazy," he says. As he was finishing his second year in law school, he was becoming more and more frustrated with himself. When he was interviewed he had completed about two-thirds of Landmark's intensive summer program. He says,

> For the first time I learned how to plan and organize my time and my materials. My tutor has worked with me to develop three-day plans. I know now how to select and highlight the points that are critical to an argument. I've learned the grammatical skills, so that there is no longer a stone wall between my ideas and my writing.

Dan returned to law school in the fall after completing the summer program. The following April, he wrote:

> After I finished at Landmark, I headed back to the University of Tulsa to resume my legal studies. But I did not leave empty-handed. The skills I learned have enabled me to have my best semester in law school. I even won the American Jurisprudence Award for excellence in Trial Advocacy.

Some students resist at first going back to the point where their knowledge and understanding break down. Mastering these skills means going back to work on exercises they consider too simple. Beth spent a year studying philosophy at a liberal arts college before she came to Landmark. She was a very bright, articulate, and thoughtful young woman, but her inability to express her knowledge in writing to reflect the depth of her understanding had led to poor grades. Beth recalls her daily battles with her Landmark tutor.

> I wanted to talk about the ideas of Heidegger and Kierkegaard, and she [my tutor] kept going back to sentence structure.

Though Beth resisted, her tutor persisted, and when Beth transferred from Landmark to a competitive four-year degree-granting college that had no special program for learning-disabled students, she was equipped to write as well as to talk. In her mid-twenties now, Beth has carved a career in the demanding field of lobbying and political campaign management.

Instructors and tutors arm their students with the skills that will allow them to face the realities of the rapidly changing world they will live in after they leave Landmark. Students come to see that the future belongs to those who know how to learn independently and to think critically. They recognize the importance of mastering the skills that allow them to access information and to communicate effectively in writing as well as in speech.

Teaching Diagnostically

Using their knowledge of how each student learns best, instructors adapt their teaching to capitalize on these strengths. Then, by observing how the student performs and what he learns, they modify their instruction. Homework is not only a means for students to practice skills and master material, it serves as a powerful diagnostic tool for teachers as well. Routinely, teachers collect and review students' work to assess their independent performance. Homework assignments thus constitute a valuable tool for planning future teaching.

Because of the emphasis on diagnostic teaching, students begin to discard the negative attitudes they have about making mistakes. They learn that each error provides a clue to understanding how they think and what they know. Mistakes, rather than being a source of shame, mark the cutting edge of their learning. They define the line that separates confusion from understanding. As teachers examine students' mistakes, they see patterns that provide them with new insights about students' learning needs. Using these insights, teachers can focus future instruction on the students' needs.

Using diagnostic teaching techniques at each step in the learning process, teachers erect a safety net that consists of three elements: (1) continuous monitoring of progress; (2) provision of regular and comprehensive feedback to students; and (3) initiating action as soon as a student falters, rather than waiting until he fails.

Committing to Hard Work and Accountability

Students who hope to succeed must work hard and be accountable for their academic progress.

> At Landmark there is no substitute for hard work. If we support one another, recognize one another's unique abilities, and commit ourselves to our common goal, the work will seem easy and the satisfaction enormous.
>
> Jim Olivier

Teachers and students at Landmark devote a great amount of time to academic tasks. A cardinal rule, reflecting the value given to these tasks, is that classes start on time and the entire class period is focused. Students are expected to be present and involved every day in all classes, as well as being up to date on all classroom and homework assignments. Each course allows only a very limited number of absences per semester, and students are required to make up missed assignments promptly.

At most traditional colleges, courses meet three hours a week; at Landmark, courses meet for four and a half hours a week. Daily homework consumes between three and five hours, and the tutorial another hour. In the intensive summer program, classes are held five and a half days per week, and include Saturday morning seminars, in which students learn about language, learning, and learning differences. It is not surprising that some students initially chafe under these demands.

> Keeping the school and my parents happy was my
> primary goal when I first came here.... I began to
> plot my course of action to get out as soon as pos-
> sible. To my surprise, my work seemed to improve,
> and for once I started to like school and what I was
> achieving.

Setting High Expectations

Students learn best when they are challenged to set their
goals high. The expectation that they will work harder
than they ever have before contributes to the results they
achieve. For this to be a positive experience, students
need teachers who are caring and knowledgeable, and
who provide a structure and sequence of instruction that
meets them where they are (Point Zero) and builds step
by step toward those goals. When these needs are met,
students gain confidence and are motivated to accept the
challenges of increasingly demanding goals.

In a world where educators often feel in competition with TV and video games, Landmark instructors
adhere to the belief that reaching challenging goals
brings its own reward. "Sugarcoating" instruction,
"watered-down" assignments, and "grade inflation" are
conspicuous by their absence.

Some students with a history of academic under-
achievement lose the sense of what they are capable of
accomplishing. Jennifer May compared her experiences
at Landmark to building a platform and looked on the
faculty and staff as holding the ladder for her as she
reached new heights.

> The job of ladder holder is a tough one. We who need
> you are always getting angry. We get angry that your
> perceptions don't fit ours, that you don't think we're
> stupid, lazy, or troublemakers. You want us to build our
> platforms higher than we think we can.

By setting increasingly more demanding goals in
classes and tutorials, Landmark instructors show students how well they can complete tasks that they struggled with in the past, such as writing a term paper or
completing a long essay examination. Students discover that goals that had seemed unattainable or unrealistic now start to come within their reach. This is a
type of chain reaction, but unlike those presented in
Chapter 4, these chain reactions are positive. They demonstrate the truth of the belief that nothing succeeds like
success.

Applying Skills Across the Curriculum

Students master skills more readily when they apply
them consistently in all their course work. When skills
instruction is limited to a single class, students often
leave what they have learned behind them as they move
on to the next class. One strength of the Landmark approach is that skills are relevant, content-based, and
applied across the curriculum. Whether in social
studies, math, biology, or history, students practice the
skills presented in the study-skills program and in their
daily tutorials.

In most schools and colleges—for reasons of scheduling, material to be covered, and the instructor's background—there is little opportunity for setting up and implementing a common set of skills practices. Each department establishes its own set of guidelines and expectations. Thus, the form in which assignments must be submitted often varies considerably from one class to another. Teachers' expectations about the quality of writing and about spelling, format, and mechanics may be vastly different. When each teacher or department sets its own guidelines in these skill-based areas, students are compelled to use several different approaches in preparing assignments. This is a problem for students who have not mastered at least one approach.

At Landmark, instructors attempt to minimize this inconsistency by working to integrate the skills across disciplines. For example, science instructors are trained in writing to ensure that writing assignments in biology receive the same degree of attention and support, and demand the same level of performance, as those done in composition class. In all academic course work, instructors strive to provide a coherent systematic approach to studying, with variations appropriate to the subject matter involved.

Additionally, within each academic department, skills specific to each course in a sequence of courses are taught explicitly and are coordinated with prior and succeeding courses. This helps ensure that students experience a progressive sequence that reinforces and builds their skills.

Learning Beyond the Classroom

Education at Landmark College extends far beyond the classroom walls. Students rub shoulders with faculty and staff throughout the day. In the dining room, residence halls, meetings, and off-campus activities, every encounter is potentially a "teachable moment." This focus on a whole learning environment was singled out for special commendation by the New England Association of Schools and Colleges accreditation team in 1991. Their report said, "The integration of in- and out-of-classroom learning is strongly exhibited."

Faculty and students engage in a continuing dialogue and learn to know and respect one another as people. Students may reveal gifts and strengths, sometimes excelling in areas not apparent in the classroom. Students have a chance to demonstrate their talents and develop their leadership skills. On a hike along the river or at a horse show, they may share thoughts and interests with their peers and their instructors. Faculty find these shared activities a natural setting for guiding students to think about social or personal issues. Or, and equally important, faculty and students may simply enjoy one another's company in an exchange that is relaxing and fun.

Success in school and in later life rests on a foundation of skills and habits that are not part of the conventional college curriculum. These include managing time, organizing, and planning. Hence, the non-academic aspects of the Landmark College program are crucial. Faculty and staff help students to make the link among the various parts of their lives, which are often viewed separately in colleges.

Believing that all experiences affect learning, Landmark College regards the seemingly diverse aspects of college life as a unit. Teamwork is central to this effort. Professors and instructors use residence-hall staff as resources, advisers consult with the admissions/diagnostic staff, teachers share effective techniques with individual students, and students play a central role in this team effort. In class and out, formal and informal practices foster teamwork and cooperation.

Understanding Oneself as a Learner

Students who know how they learn become more effective learners. From the day a student starts the admissions process until he leaves the college, he is engaged in discovering how he learns best. In an admissions interview, his counselor starts him on the road to finding out how he learns and what his special learning strengths and weaknesses are. Formal and informal assessments guide the selection of the student's academic program, his instructors and tutors, and suitable materials of instruction.

This focus on how he learns is reinforced in every course he takes, as well as in his daily sessions with his tutor. His entire program includes instruction that gives a central position to his learning style and needs. Students are encouraged to take an increasing role in discussions and planning sessions, with the goal of having them become effective self-advocates and decision makers, capable of taking charge of the process.

In a speech to the Landmark College community, one student used an analogy that clarifies the profound effect that self-awareness and understanding have on students' sense of their potential and their hope for the future.

Society is a kind of mirror, for we see ourselves through its perceptions and values. It is difficult to understand, especially when you are young, that the distortion or deficiency you see in yourself in this mirror may be partly a distortion in the mirror.

As I struggled through high school, I looked into the mirror of society's values and perceptions to see if I wasn't missing something. Was I really insufficiently dedicated to my studies? Was I a loser?

At Landmark College I found a new mirror, a new way of seeing my weaknesses and the strengths I was not sure I had. Here I finally managed to see reflected the possibility of success.

The mirror Landmark presents to its students reveals selves capable of accomplishment. This mirror gives us a truer reflection of what we are and what we can hope to accomplish through hard work. With it we escape from the distortions of a carnival house of mirrors. Learning day by day to surmount our difficulties, we may also help provide a mirror in which we may see not only our disabilities, but our immense potential as well.

Keith Promisel

APPENDIX B
Guides to Schools and Colleges

Kravets, M., and I. F. Wax. 1995. *The K & W Guide to Colleges for the Learning Disabled: A Resource Book for Students, Parents, and Professionals*. Cambridge, MA: Educators Publishing Service.

Lipkin, M. 1992. *Schoolsearch Guide to Private Schools with Programs or Services for Students with Learning Disabilities*. Belmont, MA: Schoolsearch.

Lipkin, M. 1993. *Schoolsearch Guide to Colleges with Programs or Services for Students with Learning Disabilities*. Belmont, MA: Schoolsearch.

Mangrum, C. T., and S. S. Strichart (eds.). 1994. *Peterson's Colleges with Programs for Students with Learning Disabilities*. Fourth Edition. Princeton, N.J.: Peterson's Guides.

APPENDIX
C
Organizations Providing Help for Parents, Students, and Teachers

Most of these have free or low-cost informational brochures, publish newsletters and journals, and conduct conferences.

American Speech Hearing Language Association (ASHA)
10801 Rockville Pike
Rockville, MD 20852
(301) 897-5700

Association of Educational Therapists (AET)
14852 Ventura Boulevard, Suite 207
Sherman Oaks, CA 91403
(818) 380-6895

Attention Deficit Disorder Association
P.O. Box 972
Mentor, OH 44061
(800) 487-2282

CH.A.D.D. (Children and Adults with Attention
Deficit Disorder)
499 NW 70th Avenue, Suite 308
Plantation, FL 33317
(305) 587-3700
FAX (305) 587-4599

Higher Education and the Handicapped (HEATH)
1 DuPont Circle NW, Suite 800
Washington, DC 20036-1193
(800) 544-3284

Learning Disabilities Association of America (LDA)
4156 Library Road
Pittsburgh, PA 15234
(412) 341-1515

The Learning Disabilities Network (LDN)
72 Sharp Street, Suite A-2
Hingham, MA 02043
(617) 340-5605

National Center for Learning Disabilities (NCLD)
381 Park Ave South, Suite 1420
New York, NY 10016
(212) 545-7510

National Information Center for Children and Youth
with Disabilities (NICHY)
P.O. Box 1492
Washington, DC 20013-1492
(202) 884-8200 or (800) 695-0285

The Orton Dyslexia Society (ODS)
8600 LaSalle Road, Suite 382
Baltimore MD 21204-6020
(410) 296-0232

D Magazines, Journals, and Newsletters

May be obtained through organizations listed in Appendix C unless otherwise noted

The Orton Dyslexia Society

Annals of Dyslexia. This is a scholarly journal containing articles on research into causes and treatment of dyslexia and other learning disorders and on exemplary teaching methods.

Perspectives on Dyslexia. A quarterly newsletter with articles geared toward parents and teachers, news of meetings and conferences, and reviews of recent books and audio- and videotapes.

The Learning Disabilities Network

LDN *Exchange.* A semi-annual newsletter/magazine with articles by and for learning-disabled individuals and their parents, teachers, and employers.

National Center for Learning Disabilities

Their World. An annual magazine whose primary audience consists of parents and teachers.

CH.A.D.D.

CH.A.D.D.ER. A biannual newsletter for adults with A.D.D.

CH.A.D.D.ER BOX. A monthly newsletter for children and adults with attention deficit disorders.

Learning Disabilities Association of America

LDA News Briefs. A bimonthly newsletter.

Learning Disabilities: A Multidisciplinary Journal. A semiannual publication for parents and teachers.

Other newsletters

ADDendum (Designed for adults with ADD)
c/o C.P.S.
5041-A Backlick Road
Annadale, VA 22003

ADDult News
c/o Mary Jane Johnson
ADDult Support Group
2620 Ivy Place
Toledo, OH 43613

E Books About Learning and Learning Problems

(Those marked with an asterisk are written for children and/or young adults with learning problems.)

*Abeel, Samantha. 1993. *What Once Was White*. Traverse City, MI: Hidden Bay Publishing.

Adams, Marilyn Jager. 1990. *Beginning to Read: Thinking and Learning About Print*. Cambridge, MA: The MIT Press.

*Betancourt, J. 1993. *My Name is Brain Brian*. New York: Scholastic.

Brinkerhoff, L. C., S. F. Shaw, and J. McGuire. 1993. *Promoting Postsecondary Education for Students with Learning Disabilities: A Handbook for Practitioners*. Austin, TX: Pro-Ed.

Gardner, H. 1983. *Frames of Mind: The Theory of Multiple Intelligences*. New York: Basic Books.

Gardner, H. 1993. *Multiple Intelligences: The Theory in Practice*. New York: Basic Books.

Hallowell, E. M., and J. J. Ratey. 1994. *Answers to Distraction*. New York: Pantheon Books.

Hallowell, E. M., and J. J. Ratey. 1994. *Driven to Distraction*. New York: Pantheon Books.

Healy, J. M. 1990. *Endangered Minds: Why Our Children Don't Think*. New York: Simon & Schuster.

Healy, J. M. 1987. *Your Child's Growing Mind: A Parents' Guide to Learning.* New York: Doubleday.

de Hirsch, K. 1984. *Language and the Developing Child.* Baltimore: The Orton Dyslexia Society.

*Janover, C., with Wallner, R. 1995. *The Worst Speller in Junior High.* Minneapolis: Free Spirit Publishing.

Learning Disabilities Council. 1991. *Understanding Learning Disabilities: A Parent Guide and Workbook.*

Lelewer, N. 1994. *Something's Not Right.* Acton, MA: VanderWyk and Burnham.

*Levine, M. 1993. *All Kinds of Minds: A Young Student's Book About Learning Abilities and Learning Disabilities.* Cambridge, MA: Educators Publishing Service.

Levine, M. 1994. *Educational Care: A System for Understanding Children with Learning Problems at Home and in School.* Cambridge, MA: Educators Publishing Service.

*Levine, M. 1990. *Keeping Ahead in School.* Cambridge, MA: Educators Publishing Service.

Mangrum, C. T. 1988. *College and the Learning Disabled Student.* Orlando, FL: Grune and Stratton.

Novick, B. Z., and M. M. Arnold. *Why Is My Child Having Trouble at School?: A Parent's Guide to Learning Disabilities.* New York: Villard Books.

Rawson, M. B. 1988. *The Many Faces of Dyslexia.* Baltimore: The Orton Dyslexia Society.

Rich, D. 1988. *Mega Skills: How Families Can Help Children Succeed in School and Beyond.* Boston: Houghton Mifflin Company.

Silver, L. 1993. *Dr. Larry Silver's Advice to Parents on Attention-Deficit Hyperactivity Disorder.* Washington, DC: American Psychiatric Press.

Silver, L. 1991. *The Misunderstood Child: A Guide for*

Parents of Learning Disabled Students. New York: McGraw Hill.

Smith, S. 1994. *Different Is Not Bad: A Book About Learning Disabilities*. Longmont, CO: Sopris West.

Smith, S. L. 1995. *No Easy Answers: The Learning Disabled Child at Home and at School* (revised edition). New York: Bantam Books.

Smith, S. L. 1992. *Succeeding Against the Odds: A Personal Account of Victory over Dyslexia*. New York: Washington Square Press.

Vail, P. L. 1991. *Common Ground: Whole Language and Phonics Working Together*. Rosemont, NJ: Modern Learning Press.

Vail, P. L. 1994. *Emotion: The On/Off Switch for Learning*. Rosemont, NJ: Modern Learning Press.

Vail, P. L. 1987. *Smart Kids with School Problems: Things to Know and Ways to Help*. New York: E. P. Dutton.

Vogel, S. A. 1990. *College Students with Learning Disabilities: A Handbook for College LD Students, Admissions Officers, Faculty, and Administrators*. Pittsburgh: Learning Disabilities Association.

West, T. G. 1991. *In the Mind's Eye: Visual Thinkers, Gifted People with Learning Difficulties, Computer Images, and the Ironies of Creativity*. Buffalo, NY: Prometheus Books.

Woodrich, D. L. 1994. *Attention Deficit Hyperactivity Disorder: What Every Parent Wants to Know*. Baltimore: Paul Brookes Publishing.

*Woods, J. E. 1990. *How to Succeed in College with Dyslexia*. Dallas: Semco Books.

APPENDIX F
Audiotapes and Videotapes

ASHA
The Impact of Attention Deficit Disorder on the Communicative Abilities of Children, Adolescents, and Adults. (Two cassette recordings)

Landmark College
Putney, VT
Teaching a Study Skills Program That Works. (Videotape)

National Center for Learning Disabilities
We Can Learn: Understanding and Helping Children with Learning Disabilities. (5-part video series and manual)

PBS Video
Alexandria VA
Learning Disabilities and Social Skills: Last One Picked . . . First One Picked On. (Presented by Richard Lavoie)

How Difficult Can This Be? Understanding Learning Disabilities: Frustration, Anxiety, Tension; The F.A.T. City Workshop. (Presented by Richard Lavoie)

New England Branch of The Orton Dyslexia Society (NEBODS)

Dyslexia: The Challenge and the Promise. (Video)

Index

ability testing, 6
accountability, 243–44
achievement testing, 6, 154, 160
active learning, 114, 172–74
active working memory, 105, 106, 108
  problems with, 115
advance organizers, 191–92
affixes, 55–56
agenda, daily, 191, 192
Alexander, Malcolm, 147
Americans with Disabilities Act (ADA), 166
analogies:
  memory and, 113
  visual representations and, 45–46
Ansari, Maryam, 229–30
aptitude (IQ) testing, 18, 154, 156
assessment, see testing
assessment conferences, 161–63
assessment reports, 153–54
associations, by infants and children, 29–30

athletes:
  practice requirements of, 180–81, 182
  skills of, 169–70
attention, 5, 93, 116–27
  conclusions about, 126–27
  energy allocation and focus-shifting function of, 118, 120–21
  functions of, 118–26
  meaning of, 117
  memory and, 109
  other learning problems and, 123–24
  previewing, monitoring and checking function of, 118, 121–22
  regulating function of, 118, 122–26
  selecting and filtering function of, 118–20
attention deficit hyperactivity disorder (ADHD; attention deficit disorder; ADD), 123–26
audiotapes about learning and learning problems, 258
auditory discrimination, 53, 62
auditory memory, short-term, 109–10

About the Authors

Carolyn Olivier, former Director of Admissions at Landmark College, participated in planning for and establishment of the college. She has developed practices and procedures in the Admissions Office to support the goals of the college. Her work in this process inspired this book and is particularly reflected in the sections of the book dealing with the ways in which we learn.

Rosemary Bowler, for many years a public school teacher and principal with a special interest in students who learn differently, more recently has served as Executive Director of The Orton Dyslexia Society and as Editor of *The Annals of Dyslexia*. Currently she is Executive Editor of the Learning Disabilities Network.